GRACE FOR PURPOSE AND THANKSGIVING

Prayers for the Week

LAVERN POWELL

Grace for Purpose and Thanksgiving
Copyright © 2021 by Lavern Powell

Publisher
LJP Publishing
www.ljppublishing.com

First Edition
978-1-7399603-0-8 – Ebook
978-1-7399603-1-5 - Paperback

Publishing Consultants
Vike Springs Publishing Ltd.
www.vikesprings.com

Printed in the
United Kingdom and United States of America
For bookings and speaking engagements, contact us:
lavern@ljppublishing.com

Lavern's books are available at special discounts when purchased in bulk for promotions or as donations for educational and training purposes.

Limit of Liability/
Disclaimer of Warranty

DEDICATION

This book is dedicated to my children; Nadia, Damion, Jadeen and Jada, and also my grandchildren, and all those who will find solace and comfort through the prayers within this book.

ACKNOWLEDGEMENTS

"When God decides to bless you, He will turn all situations to be in your favour." I am grateful to the Almighty Father in His wisdom and strength for making all things possible in my life. I would like to take this opportunity to acknowledge the following people for their support, prayers, songs and inspiration to help me fulfil this purpose: my family who has inspired me with their encouragement and help in writing this book. Andrea Ferguson Oakley, my friend and sister for over 40 Years, she has been my rock, my inspiration, my back bone throughout the years, Mrs Winsome Baugh a dear friend, for your encouragement, love and appreciation, and the Turner sisters Carla and Brigette, for your friendship throughout the years. Premier Gospel FM – I can't start the day without listening to you; the songs, the Spirit Charge, the word of God, and the Bible verses, which uplift me every day. Thank you to the Rev. Peter Davis from the station for the songs he played throughout the night, and Belinda Brooks for her continued inspiration. Thank you to the Praying Mums Whatsapp Group – Rosita Ero, Grace Bjabiamila for their prayers and support. My great friend Glenda Bennett – for her support throughout my spiritual journey, and her encouragement. Place of Grace (POG), Pastor Timothy Ramsey, and his wife Adwoa Ramsey for their prayers, teaching, love, and encouragement. Thank you to Victor Kwegyir and his team for their professional service, editing, designing, printing, marketing, and worldwide distribution; you all have contributed in many different ways to make this possible for me. I APPRECIATE YOU!

INTRODUCTION

"THE MOST WONDERFUL PLACE TO BE IN THE MORNING IS IN SOMEONE'S HEART, THOUGHTS, AND PRAYERS." This prayer book was born out of my yearning to draw closer to God, and dwell on His words. If it wasn't for waking up each morning, and giving God thanks, I wouldn't be alive to testify about God's goodness and mercy in my Life. One morning in 2018, I was in a Road Traffic Collision (RTC). I witnessed the Hand of God descend and shift the van that was going to crush me to death. A voice followed that said, "I'M NOT DONE WITH YOU YET." Tears came streaming down my face knowing that God had saved my life. Since then, I have been having daily conversations with God, attending church, and asking Him to show me my purpose. It follows that I began sending out daily prayers on Whatsapp. However, deep down I knew God had added assignments for me. Hence, I sought instruction from Him on praying. I may not possess the skills to make a public presentation, however, I asked God to show me another way to connect with His people. This book is the end result. Since then I have risen each day at 5.00 a.m. to deliver God's blessings through the power of prayer. The prayers of the Holy Spirit involve reaching out to people and inspiring them in their daily lives. For example, this book will help readers build their faith and develop a better prayer regimen with God. It will also shed light on their Christian journey, as well inspire a little soul-searching.

OUR GOD IS ABLE AND HE IS IN CONTROL!

Week One

1. A New Beginning

Philippians 4:13:

"I can do all things through Christ who strengthens me."

Heavenly Father, thank you for bringing us to a brand new day and week. We bless your holy name! We thank you for your mercy and grace which woke us up this morning and kept us safe throughout the night. We remain forever grateful for our families, friends, homes and jobs, and pray that you will send angels to protect us, and our loved ones today. May you mend every broken heart, touch all who need healing, comfort all who mourn and bless those with financial needs.

In the precious name of Jesus... THANK GOD...

Amen.

NOTES

_____

_____

_____

_____

Jeremiah 29:11:

"For I know the plans I have for you, declares the Lord, plans to prosper you not to harm you, plans to give you hope and a future..."

Thank you, Lord for another day. We know not what today may bring, but you do, Lord. We put our lives in your hands and move forward in our day. Father, we face today trials and tribulations, but in the midst of all this we know that you are Lord and saviour. Help us to be at peace and put aside all anxious thought, and let us not forget that you are our strength, and shield, you are not only with us, but in us, and in Him.

We bless your name forever, and thank you for keeping us covered under the blood of Jesus.

In your name we do pray... THANK GOD...

Amen.

NOTES

God promises in Isaiah 54:11 that He will rebuild the city that is lashed by storms with precious stones. Life brings us many storms and it can feel unsettling, and without comfort at these times. When we make a commitment to follow Jesus, we allow God to start a process in us where He can rebuild us from those storms. But this is not an easy process; we have to lay a foundation and allow God to begin those changes in us.

Prayer

Thank you, Father, that you can rebuild our lives, and that when storms lash us, you are our comforter. We pray that however hard the process of rebuilding our foundations is, we remain open to this so we can be a new creation that will shine for you... In Jesus' name... THANK GOD...

Amen.

NOTES

_____

_____

_____

_____

_____

Heavenly Father, in the mighty name of Jesus, thank you for another day. Thank you for your love, joy, strength and mercy, because you are an amazing and awesome God, and you have been so good to us. We are beyond blessed. Help us today to walk in your power and your peace. We declare we walk in victory that we find in you, we cannot be overtaken, nor shall we be moved. You are so amazing, Lord God.

Today we ask you to move on behalf of your people who find themselves trapped in certain situations, whether that be a bad relationship, financial troubles, or even family difficulties. Release them, dear God, and let them walk in victory, bind the works of the enemy, break every chain that needs to be broken. Set them free, Lord God, as we know the chains were broken at calvary, and we are set free. We give you all the praise, honour and glory because it's already yours. In the mighty name of Jesus... THANK GOD...

Amen.

NOTES

Good morning, Father God, thank you for the breath of life on another day you have made, we will be glad and rejoice in it. Today we ask that you walk with us, not just today but throughout our life; lead and guide us and keep us forever lifted up into your righteous hand. Give us the strength and the health we need to carry any heavy burdens that are placed upon our shoulder; we know we can cast all our cares upon your shoulders, Lord, you never leave us nor forsake us. Have your divine ways for each and every one of us individually, and let your will be done in our lives when our heart and mind is unsettled. Fill us with your peace so we may experience unspeakable joy around all things.

Father God, surround each and every one of us with your presence. Help us to focus our values and what really matters in our lives, but most importantly let us focus on what you have done for us, Lord God – not complaining over what we have or don't have. Let us be thankful for all the good you have shown us, what you have done, and what you are about to do in our lives. We only have to reach out to you, Lord Jesus, you're never too busy to hear us. We thank you because you are our God, our peace, our saviour, and we give you all the praise, honour and glory because it's already yours. In Jesus' name we pray. THANK GOD...

Amen.

NOTES

Week Two

1. Walking in His Presence

As you go forth in His presence this week, I decree that the God that honours and that no man can reverse shall prove Himself strong in your life. I declare that there shall be performance of God's words in your life. As you can never again see yesterday in life, so also you will never again see failure, disappointment, sickness, pains and sorrow in Jesus' name. As you see today, all round favour, open doors, good health, long life and prosperity shall be yours. As you expect tomorrow, all your expectations in life will come to pass in Jesus' precious name...THANK GOD...

Amen.

NOTES

_____

_____

_____

_____

Lord, you're good and your mercies endures forever. We love you, we magnify you, we praise you, we honour you this morning. Thank you for determination, purpose, for the issue and the problem, and for the things that make us better. Thank you, God, for working through us to help us be better and to do better. Show us ourselves, God, when we're heading in the wrong direction, where we are stepping wrong, and thinking wrong. Show us ourselves so we live right, not for people, but for you and ourselves. Help us to be honest whether we're in pain, or whether we are feeling victorious. Help us to not lie about our emotions, and feelings.

Lord, we know you care about the broken-hearted, you care about our ups and down, our tears, our pain, and we want to get to a better place, so we thank you, God; we surrender all to you, every problem, pain, issue, care and concern. Before we save the world, Lord God, help us to save ourselves, because we can do it through your power, grace, and mercy. We love you, God, we magnify you, we thank you; you've done great things before and you will do so again. You have blessed us before, and you will do it again, Lord. You have brought us out before, and you will bring us out again. We declare that our family is well, our children are safe and healthy, our money is fine, our parents are good. We give you glory and honour for being the protector that we need. In Jesus' name... THANK GOD...

Amen.

NOTES

Father, in the mighty name of Jesus we thank you and we praise you for another day. Thank you for waking us up to see the sunrise, and for carrying us through another week. Sustain and keep each of us in your will, and allow us to surrender to you anything that is unlike you. Thank you for purpose and destiny, thank you for the passion to do the right thing, thank you for the drive that you place in each and every one of us.

Lord God, reignite that fire in each and every one of us, stir up that gift in us; the gift that will bless the nation, give glory, and will leave a legacy for our children and families. Help us to be diligent and move forward towards to what you have placed inside of us, help us not to let our dreams die, Father. We thank you for mending broken hearts, we thank you for bringing strategy, and wisdom for the things that will bring change to the world and our lives – things that may be difficult, but we got the strength to do them through you, Lord God. We praise you, glorify, and magnify you, we thank you for the abundance that's coming. We cast out the spirit of fear, sickness, doubt, and anger. Lord, we give you all the praise, honour and glory. In your name, Jesus... Hallelujah... THANK GOD...

Amen.

NOTES

8

4. A New Day

Heavenly Father, we thank you for carrying us through another night with your guardian angels protecting us. Thank you for giving us strength through all the anguish and tears of yesterday; whatever trials and struggles we are going to face today, we know with you we will find our strength. You are the most high God, we worship, praise, and love you, God. Lord, go before us and clear our way; we have our own plan for the day and we ask that you guide every decision that we make. May your angels watch over each and every one of us wherever we go, whatever situation we are in. As we come to you today, Father, knowing all power is in your hands, fill us up with more of your love, peace, and joy. Increase in our life as we diminish, carry us over all stumbling blocks and barriers, and please shine on and through us, so that everyone can see you are the all-powerful God, who is directing our ways. Father, give us rest when we are weary, and renew our spirit and our strength when we feel troubled in our mind, heart, body and soul, reminding us that it is only you who has the power to get us through all things beyond our control. Thank you for knowing that we can rely on you in all things. In Jesus' mighty name... THANK GOD...

Amen.

NOTES

Lord, we thank you for this morning, and we give you all the glory and praise. Thank you for waking us up to another sunrise, because you are the God of miracles and wonders. We give you all the praise and glory. Help us to put our hope and trust in you, and no one else; you are our everything. Thank you, Lord, for saving our soul, and making us whole, and for giving us salvation. Teach us how to cope with all the worries, doubts, fears, insecurities, and uncertainties we are going to face today, for your word says in John 14:1 "Let not our hearts be troubled".

We appreciate you, Father God, for being our rock, our fortress, our shield, and our strong tower. Your grace is never failing; even when we fall you are there to pick us up. We are letting go today, Lord Jesus, so take full control, we seek you for direction. Thank you for being beside us every step of the way, on our journey through this precious life that we are so blessed to have, to live, to breathe, and be. We give you all the honour. In your precious name, Jesus... THANK GOD...

Amen.

NOTES

_____

_____

_____

_____

Week Three

1. Add to One's Faith

Heavenly Father, we call upon you this morning on bended knees, because you're good and your mercies endure forever. We thank you and we praise you for another day. We thank you, Lord God, for giving us strength, wisdom, favour, grace, and mercy. Your scripture told us to add to one's faith; help us to do the work we need to do, to add long suffering and diligence, and help us remember that we have the responsibility in this. Help us choose to do the right thing, choose to serve, love, forgive, stand for righteousness, and justice in the name of Jesus.

We thank you, God, for wisdom, favour, and grace. We thank you that you are changing and shifting the world as we see it; it will never be the same, and you are using us to do it, so we will stand tall as soldiers in the army of the Lord. Your army does not lose, your army does not fail, you are with us and for us, and not against us. We thank you, and praise you for the victory that is ours because your ways are not man's way. In Jesus' name we pray... THANK GOD...

Amen.

NOTES

Lord, we thank you and we praise you for another day. When we are awake, we know we are still with you; we thank you and we give you all the praise, you're a mighty and sovereign God. Lord, we know we're going to face challenges and struggles today; we pray that you help each of us to remain focused on you. Keep a guard over our mouth, and let us not incline our hearts toward any evil thing. Help us to have a spirit of gratitude, as we face the twists and turns of life, to see the good in the bad, and the happy in the sad. Grant us a cheerful spirit to do whatever needs to be done when things don't go our way. Help us not to lean on our own understanding, but in everything acknowledge you so you can direct our words, thoughts and actions when trials come into our path.

Lord, as we rise and face each day, help us to embrace whatever happens. Give us strength, wisdom, and courage to get through all challenges and hardship, and most importantly, help us to reflect and live out our life in a way pleasing to you. Help each of us live a life that brings honour to your holy name, and as we face tough choices, and hard solutions, help us to remember that we are your children, and can always trust and believe in you for our miracles. In your name we pray...THANK GOD...

Amen.

NOTES

3. The Lord is My Shepherd

The Lord is my shepherd; I shall not want. He maketh me to lie down in green pastures: he leadeth me beside the still waters. He restoreth my soul: He leadeth me in the paths of righteousness for His name's sake. Yea, though I walk through the valley of the shadow of death, I will fear no evil, for thou art with me; thy rod and thy staff they comfort me. Thou preparest a table before me in the presence of mine enemies: thou anointest my head with oil; my cup runneth over. Surely goodness and mercy shall follow me all the days of my life, and I will dwell in the house of the Lord forever... THANK GOD...

Amen.

NOTES

4. Renew Our Hearts

Father, in the mighty name of Jesus, we give you thanks and praise for today. You're an awesome and mighty God. The alarm clock didn't wake us up this morning, but through your grace and mercy we arise into your light. Renew our hearts and minds for all the days ahead. Firmly plant your words of truth within us, keeping us focused on what is pure, right and obedient to your word. We know that your voice speaks louder and stronger, and your plans will not fail us.

Father, we pray for you to be our defender, our protector in keeping our pathways clear, removing all obstacles, and covering all pitfalls. Keep us on your level ground, and let your light shine in, through, and over us along the way. Help us to make a difference in this world for your glory and purposes, so we may live in gladness all the days of our precious life. Thank you, Father, for your words continue to lead us, so we give you all the glory and praise. In the mighty and precious name of Jesus... THANK GOD...

Amen.

NOTES

Father, in the mighty name of Jesus we lift up your name, and give you all the praise this morning, because we made it to the end of another week. Lord Jesus, we lift our hands to tell you that we love you always, and through the storms of life we live on your promise that you will never leave us nor forsake us. The enemy will come, but we know we have the victory, as your word says in Psalms 34:19: "Many are the afflictions of the righteous, but the Lord delivers us out of them all".

You are working for us right now, you created us for a purpose, and you have a perfect plan for our life. We ask that you fulfil your purpose for us, and help us to do our part by seeking you each and every day. Father, use our trials to strengthen us from our "what if" faith to a "no matter what" faith. We pray for healing and grace to cover everyone, every broken place, every wound, and every heartache. May your divine presence never depart from us today and throughout the coming weeks. Empower us to overcome everything, purify our hearts, and set us apart for your glory. In your mighty, holy and precious name, Jesus...THANK GOD...

Amen.

NOTES

Week Four

1. Prayer for a New Week

Our Father, we thank you for this day, for this is your day, the day you have made, and we will be glad and rejoice in it. Father we commit this new week to you, we give you all the praise and glory. Father, thank you for the divine opportunities you're opening in our lives this week. God, we lift up everyone to you this morning in the mighty name of Jesus. God, you said that if we call on you, you will answer. Thank you for your favour and blessings on our lives. Today and for the rest of this week, we choose to live in excellence and do everything to the best of our abilities. Lord, as we are in this new week, we give you all the glory, praise, honour. We thank you in advance for being with us throughout the week, through our trials, tribulations, and decisions. You never leave us, Lord God, and for this we are so grateful. Fill us with the hopes and desires that you have in store for us. Grant us divine wisdom to make the right decisions in all we do, with the guidance of your holy spirit. We can do all things through Christ who loves us. In the mighty name of Jesus... THANK GOD...

Amen.

NOTES

2. A Prayer for Our Families and Friends

Heavenly and most gracious Father, you are the Alpha and Omega. You are the Almighty God from beginning to the end, you never leave us nor forsake us. Thank you for being the watchkeeper through our night's rest, and for waking us to another day of sunrise. As your word goes out, we pray that it goes out with healing, power and precision, fill our mouths with good this week.

We know you are a good God, and you have good plans for us. We all need your special attention, and we pray to you to deliver us from any paths of destruction. Fulfil your plans for our lives, and lead each of us in the way of righteousness. Help us to keep our faith, and to be obedient to your word, so that we may flourish in peace and extend our days on this earth you've created.

Father, today please bless our families and friends; where there is hatred, show them LOVE, where there is sorrow, give them COMFORT, where there is sadness bring JOY. But overall, Father we pray you give them your PEACE, and your STRENGTH, to get through it all. We thank you for all our blessings – the roof over our head, food, clothing, the family we love, and most of all the precious gift of life. Open our eyes and hearts, dear Lord that we may know you more fully. In Jesus' name we pray... THANK GOD...

Amen.

NOTES

3. A Declaration

My life is a bundle of joy and happiness, for the joy of the Lord is my strength! Irrespective of my circumstances, I remain blessed, cheerful, and boisterous with praise, knowing that I draw out prosperity, peace, success, health, and other blessings from deep within me... Glory to God!!!

Prayer

Heavenly Father, in the mighty name of Jesus, thank you for making a way, where at times there seems to be no way. We believe that with you all things are possible! Show us your power today; work through us. Father, thank you for empowering us to live in victory today; we know all victory belongs to you, and with you we find our strength. Help us to live a life that is pleasing to you and glorifies your holy name. Father, we surrender our hearts, minds, will and emotions to you, so we can live as a testimony of your work. We hunger for every single thing you have in store for us. Thank you for leading and guiding us this week. In Jesus' name... THANK GOD... Amen.

NOTES

God helps those who seek Him! Lord, we lift up our eyes unto the hills from whence comes our help. Our help comes from the Lord who made heaven and earth. He will not allow our foot to be moved: He who keeps us will not slumber. Behold, He who keeps Israel shall neither slumber nor sleep. The Lord is our keeper; the Lord is our shade at our right hand. The sun shall not strike us by day, nor the moon by night. The Lord shall preserve us from all evil, He shall preserve our soul. The Lord shall preserve our going out and our coming in, from this time forth, and even for evermore... THANK GOD...

Amen.

NOTES

Heavenly Father, thank you for taking us through another week; we made it, Lord Jesus, through you. Lord, no matter what we face today, with your help we will endure, overcome and prevail. May every evil plan of the enemy fail, because you are our faithful provider, and protector, and we are so grateful. We declare that you are worthy, holy and you are the centre of our joy, peace and strength. Thank you for your abundant promises; we will rise higher in you, and we can do all things because you give us strength. Thank you, God, now and in advance for the way that you provide for all our needs, whether we recognise it or not. In your holy spirit and your name we pray... THANK GOD...

Amen.

NOTES

Week Five

1. A Prayer of Praise

Heavenly Father, thank you for another week to worship and praise your holy name. Father, your word says, "Let everything that has breath praise the Lord!" Let our praises go up to your heavenly throne today as a sweet-smelling saviour. Lord, we dedicate each day of this new week to your powerful hand. Let this coming week be our week of divine encounter. Come into our hearts, Holy Spirit, and take total control. Let chains be broken, mountains be levelled, bodies be healed, dark clouds dispersed and doors of favour opened for us, in the mighty name of Jesus.

Father, increase us on every side this week and grant us your divine wisdom, knowledge and understanding. We ask for your favour to break new ground. We declare and believe that no evil shall come near our dwelling, our family, work, our body or our thoughts. Thank you, Father, for your divine protection, and deliver us safely in our going out and coming in each day. In Jesus' mighty name we pray... THANK GOD...

Amen.

NOTES

Romans 8:28:

"For we know that all things work together for good to those who love God, to those who are called according to His purpose."

Heavenly Father, thank you for this new day in you. Thank you for your love, grace, and mercy. Thank you for your wisdom and insight. Thank you for watching over us, and for making a way for us. Father, our hope and trust are in you. We ask that you do what you can do in and through our lives.

Heavenly Father, thank you for your faithfulness even when we are unfaithful. Thank you for drawing us close to you when we feel discouraged. Today, we choose to lift up our eyes to you, for you are our source of strength and help. You are the author and finisher of our faith. Father, today we choose to trust you. We release every frustration over the dreams and desires in our hearts because you know what's best for us. Grant us the patience to wait upon you, Lord. We choose to trust your timing, knowing that you are faithful. We will bless you in all things and at all times. In Jesus' mighty name we pray... THANK GOD...

Amen.

NOTES

_____

_____

_____

1 John 4:18:

"There is no fear in love; but perfect love cast out fear, because fear involves torment. But he who fears has been made perfect in love."

Most gracious and Heavenly Father, we thank you for your blessings upon our lives. Thank you for this new day in you. Protect and guide us throughout this day. Thank you for loving us and guiding us, because there's no greater love than you. Father, you will never give up on us, as we stand on your word. You'll never leave, nor forsake us. Help us to remember that we are safe in your strong hand. Father, we love you, and we exalt you. We trust you and we believe you, and we need you. There's no one and nothing that compares to you, your goodness, your love, and your grace. Right now, Father, we surrender all. We submit to your authority. Father, we ask that you continue to rule and reign in our lives. Touch those who are hurting, and going through hard times, give them comfort, let them know they don't need to fear tomorrow, for you are the same God who loves us each and every day. Help us not to give up on you, because you won't give up on us. We give you all the praise, honour and glory, and let your holy spirit lead the way. In Jesus' name... THANK GOD...

Amen.

NOTES

Lord Jesus, we thank you for your love, power and protection. Heavenly Father, thank you for the many blessings you've given us. How thankful we are for the Holy Spirit and your precious word, which you use to set us free from worry. Father God, we ask that you make all things anew in our hearts, in our minds and in our lives, so that your words of truth are forever planted firm within us, and we pray that you keep our footsteps firm on your solid foundation so that we are safe with you.

We ask for your healing touch for all of your people today. Heal their bodies, minds and their souls. Lay your hand upon them today and free them from any fear or anxiety that may be disrupting their lives and families. We know it is only through you, Lord, that they will have peace. Bless all of your people today as the Holy Spirit continues to lead our way. In Jesus' name we pray... THANK GOD...

Amen.

NOTES

_____

_____

_____

_____

Hebrews 12:2:

"Looking unto Jesus, the author and finisher of our faith, who for the joy that was set before him endured the cross, despising the shame, and has sat down at the right hand of the throne of God."

Powerful Father, we humbly come before your presence this morning, thanking you for being our watchkeeper throughout the night, and for waking us to another day, and taking us through another week. Heavenly Father, we humbly come to you today. We ask that you help us stay focused on eternal things this coming weekend. We declare that we have joy and peace today, no matter what comes our way, because we know we have the ultimate victory in you.

Father, thank you for your word which is a lamp to our feet and a light to our path. Today, we meditate on your truth which is our source of strength and faith. Help us to be stable-minded, as we set our focus on you. We invite you to have your way in our lives. Remove anything that would hold us back from all you have in store for us today and this weekend. We are counting on you, Lord, and we put our hope in your word. Keep us lifted with your righteous hand, and please be the strength that we need to cope, with hope, knowing that in your perfect time and in your perfect way you will bring us through this day. We love, worship, and adore you, Father. In Jesus' mighty name we pray... THANK GOD...

Amen.

NOTES

Week Six

1. Strengthen Our Faith

Philippians 4:13:

"I can do all things through Christ who strengthens me."

Lord, we just want to thank you for who you are, and for what you do. Continue to make us better and strengthen your words into us so our faith can be strengthened through you. Another beautiful morning we're here to see, and we thank you, Lord Jesus. Today we ask that you renew our minds by the word of God so that our thoughts are your thoughts. Teach us to enjoy our relationships more because they are all that matter in eternity. Help us to enjoy the journey of life as our path shines brighter and brighter throughout this day and the week ahead of us. Help us to love others the way you have commanded. Give us the strength to walk in your ways and understand your love more. Give us that inner peace, Lord, so we can restore all the joy that you have for us. Help us to believe in your promises which are true, and walk with patience. We know you will continue to watch, provide, shield, protect, heal and deliver us because you love us. In Jesus' mighty name we pray... THANK GOD...

Amen.

NOTES

Psalms 46:1:

"God is our refuge and strength, a very present help in trouble."

Heavenly Father God, thank you for the gift of life. Thank you that you are the master planner, and everything you say and do is perfect. Thank you for being with us as we go through this day. Help us to keep our mind stayed on you, Lord Jesus, because you will keep us in perfect peace.

Father, today we choose to forget the past. We don't want anything to hold us back from the good plans you have prepared for us. Father, search our hearts today and see if there is anything that is keeping us from walking in unity with other believers. We choose love today. We choose peace. Help us to be an example of your love to those around us. Meet each of us at our point of need today. Make a way where there appears to be none. Open new doors for us. Close doors that no longer need to be open. We praise you because you are the Prince of Peace. In Jesus' mighty name we pray... THANK GOD...

Amen.

NOTES

_____

_____

_____

Genesis 39:3:

"The Lord shall bless whatever you do. When you involve him, he can take even your mistakes and turn them around for good."

Heavenly Father, we praise, bless and adore you. You are the Kings of Kings, and Lord above all. We magnify your name because you are great, and there's no one like you. We thank you for the gift of life this morning. Thank you for your goodness and for the blessings you have in store for us. As we journey through the week, we declare that your steadfast love never ceases. Your mercies never come to an end. They are new every morning; great is thy faithfulness, O Lord!

Thank you, Father for new blessings, new grace, new mercies, new favour and new provisions. We release any doubt and confusion to you. Help us to focus on your word which is truth that sets us free. Guide us in the way that we should go as we stay focused on you and planted in your word. Give us a sincere and blameless heart that we may serve you all the days of our lives. In Jesus' mighty name we pray... THANK GOD...

Amen.

NOTES

Lamentations 3:22-24:

"Through the Lord's mercies we are not consumed, Because HIS compassion fail not. They are new every morning; Great is your faithfulness."

Father God, thank you for waking us up to this new day. We are blessed and glad to be alive. We thank you that you hold the victory over sin and death in this world. Thank you for the redemptive work you are doing in our lives, and for the freedom and hope that you bring, knowing that more goodness is yet to come for each and every one of us.

Heavenly Father, today we stand in faith and invite you to move mightily on our behalf. Help us to stand strong against the wicked plans of the enemy and learn to walk in love always. Today we release every care, concern, offence and disappointment to you. We choose to keep the peace that you have given us. Father, it is our hearts' desire to know you and to be known by you. Help us to live the life you've called us to and be faithful to you. We ask that your Holy Spirit be with us and lead us. Let the words of our mouths and the meditations of our hearts be pleasing to you each day of this week and month. In Jesus' mighty name we pray.THANK GOD...

Amen.

NOTES

Lord, we thank you and praise you for another day. We thank you for bringing us to the end of another week. It's your love and mercy that has brought us through, and we thank you for always loving us, despite our mistakes.

Heavenly Father, we receive your grace today, which is your supernatural empowerment. We release guilt and condemnation, and we receive your love and forgiveness. Search our hearts, O God. Renew us and cleanse us by your word. Father, thank you for your mercy upon our lives. Thank you for empowering us to rise above every obstacle. We trust that you are moving us forward into the victory you have for us. Draw us close to you and empower us by your Holy Spirit this weekend, to fulfil the dreams and destiny that you have placed within us. In Jesus' mighty name we pray...THANK GOD...

Amen.

NOTES

Week Seven

1. Only by Your Grace

Psalms 66:19-20:

"But certainly God had heard me; He has attended to the voice of my prayer. Blessed be God, who has not turned away my prayer, nor his mercy from me."

Heavenly Father, we thank you for bringing us safely and healthily to this new week. We acknowledge that it's only by your grace that we have made it this far, and for that we say thank you, God, for neither leaving us nor forsaking us. Thank you for your blessing upon our lives. Thank you for watching over us, shielding, protecting, and providing for us. You are a good God, and your mercy has renewed for us today. Father, we surrender our hearts, our wills, minds and emotions to you. Today and this new week we lift our hearts to you, trusting that your light will burst forth through the darkness in our lives. Renew, revive and restore us again. Father, we release the past. We let go of the good and the bad. Search our hearts. Show us any area where we need to make adjustments so that we can move forward and upward with you in this new week. In Jesus' mighty name we pray. THANK GOD...

Amen.

NOTES

Psalms 100:3:

"Know that the Lord, He is God; It is He who has made us, and not we ourselves, we are his people and the sheep of His pasture."

Eternal and Heavenly Father, you are our first response in all we do. This is the day you've made and we will be glad and rejoice in it. We will bless and magnify your name at all times, and your praise will continually be in our mouth, all day long. Today we will think positive, we will focus on all that is good, and remove all doubt and fear.

We will not dwell on what has happened, but what is coming. Help us to look forward, and let our faith, and your Holy Spirit lead the way. Thank you for the answers, healing and directions to come. We thank you that you guide us and guard us; keep us in the centre of your will and the palm of your hands, Lord. Those who are struggling, Lord God, give them extra strength; those who are dealing with tough things, God, help them to just keep the faith and hang in there with you, because faith will lead us home. We give you praise, glory, and honour for every blessing. In Jesus' name we pray... THANK GOD...

Amen.

NOTES

Psalms 61:1-3:

"Hear my cry, O God; Attend to my prayer. From the end of the earth, I will cry to You. When my heart is overwhelmed; Lead me to the rock that is higher than I. For you have been a shelter for me, a strong tower from the enemy."

Heavenly Father, thank you for another day in which to see your goodness in our lives. Thank you for pouring out your favour and blessing upon us. Empower us by your Holy Spirit to fulfil your plan for our lives. Let your flame burn brightly into us now and forevermore.

Father, today we come to you believing you have given us the victory. We will not focus on the obstacles before us today; instead, we will focus on you. We give you all the praise, honour, and glory, because it's already yours. In Jesus' mighty name we pray... THANK GOD...

Amen.

NOTES

_____

_____

_____

_____

Psalms 56:3:

"Whenever I'm afraid, I will trust in You."

Dear God, thank you for waking us up to see another sunrise. So many didn't live to see this day but I'm glad we did. For this is the day you've made, and we will be glad and rejoice in it.

Father God, right now we take time to remember and acknowledge your goodness in our lives. We praise you because you are good. Help us to stay filled with your joy so we can serve you with our whole hearts in everything that we do. Father, thank you for making us alive in Christ! We declare that Jesus is our Lord and saviour, and because He died for us, we can live the abundant life here on earth. Help us stay focused on you this day and live with the enthusiasm that comes from knowing you. Lord, we pray that you continue to extend your arms of love to us, and each of our family members, and members of all families. We ask that you guide our words, our ways of thinking and actions so that we are able to push through whatever happens. Help us to seek directions from you and surrender all to you because we know change will come. We give you all the praise and honour today. In Jesus' mighty name we pray... THANK GOD...

Amen.

NOTES

5. The Gift of the Morning

Lord, the greatest gift you give us this morning is our eyes, that are open to see another day. Thank you for taking us through another week. Father, we thank you because you are the God who fights our battles. Thank you for your love and grace that are ours. Lord, today we let go of all the hurts, offences, and wounds of the past. We declare that they have no power over us today. Lord, we put our nation before you this morning, we are still fighting this unseen evil spirit. We ask for your help as we approach your throne of grace, fully aware that you are our only hope. We are grateful for your Holy Spirit and precious word which you use to set us free from fear. We know you have been with us through all the storms, and we trust that you already know what is needed. Keep us forever focused on you, and keep our hearts steadfastly trusting you. Teach us to be content and humble, help us to endure and persevere through all our trials and tribulations. Lord, we just want to take the time to say thank you. In Jesus' name we pray... THANK GOD...

Amen.

NOTES

Week Eight

1. The Lord is Our Light

Heavenly Father, we thank you, love, and praise you. You are so good and your mercies endure forever. We thank you for the victory you've given to us. We thank you that this victory will go with us throughout this week, and we will rest, trust and stand on your word. We speak life, and speak faith, God, we can do all things through Christ who loved us. We can go through all tests and beat any problems. Lord God, with you we can do all things. We thank you for guarding and covering us, for keeping us safe from all hurt, harm and dangers. We understand you move by our faith, but not our fear, so help us to speak in faith and declare all goodness over our life. We ask that you block the devil, and cancel the assignment of the evil that the enemy is putting on us. Let the angels of protection guard and cover us, keep us safe and healthy. Keep us filled with your joy and your peace.

Someone is going through difficult times today, Lord. We thank you for healing their mind and their heart, being just what they need, right when they need it. Have your ways in our life and we praise your name forever more. THANK GOD...

Amen.

NOTES

2. The Mercy of God

There is no door that the mercy of God cannot open. He opened Bartholomew's blind eyes, opened Elizabeth's barren womb, opened the Red Sea for the Israelites and terminated 430 years of slavery. As you rise up this morning, we pray that all the angels of help and mercy rise up and work for us. May every door of blessings, joy, happiness, prosperity, salvation and every good thing shut against us be opened. May our lives attract mercy and favour in Jesus' mighty name...THANK GOD...

Amen.

NOTES

Heavenly Father, we thank you for purpose, strength, and destiny. We asked you to be with us all day long, and you let us feel your presence, God. You are our hiding place and under your wings we can always find refuge.

Heavenly Father, today we rejoice in you because in all things, at all times, in every circumstance we will praise you.

God, we release what we cannot control into your hands today. We submit ourselves to you and thank you for the victory in every area of our lives. Father, today we will hold on to joy, no matter our present circumstances! We will live each day with your peace and happiness, relying on your strength and your word. You are the God from whom all of our help comes. You are our protector, provider, peace, our guide, our shelter and our hope. You are our refuge and strength; our light and our salvation. For if you be for us who can be against us? Today, no matter what comes our way, we know, believe and confess that we are more than conquerors through Christ Jesus... THANK GOD...

Amen.

NOTES

Romans 8:28:

"And we know that all things work together for good to those who love God, to those who are called according to his purpose..."

Lord, we thank you, praise, love, and glorify your name. Thank you for brand new mercies, and opportunities for this day. Lord Jesus, because you loved us you have provided everything we need through the cross. We have abundant life, we have divine health, and we have your unmerited favour.

Heavenly Father, today we praise you because you are worthy! Thank you for your faithfulness. Thank you for your love. Thank you for provision, healing, strength and joy. Thank you for abundantly supplying all our needs according to your riches in glory. Thank you for revealing your plans and purposes for us as we go down into the deep waters of life. Thank you for refreshing and renewing our hearts. Help us to do good and stand firm until we see our harvest of blessing. Thank you for your victory to reign over every area of our lives. We receive every blessing you have for us today. In Jesus' mighty name we pray. THANK GOD...

Amen.

NOTES

Lord, we lift your name on high this morning, because you are a merciful and wonderful God, no matter who we are. You've taken us through another week, and woke us up to see the light of today. For this we are grateful!

Heavenly Father, today we lift up our eyes to you. We accept and believe your every word by faith. We believe you will complete the good work you've started in our lives. Thank you for making us righteous in Christ and help us to follow you all the days of our lives. God, help us to be a testimony of your love and forgiveness to those around us.

Father, today we thank you for bringing to pass the dreams in our hearts. Thank you for new beginnings as we walk every day with you. We invite your plan to unfold in our lives today. We open our hearts and minds to you and declare that Jesus is Lord over us. Bless each and every one under the sound of our voice, keep us in the centre of your will and the palm of your hand today. Open doors that are closed, make all the decisions for us, Lord God, and make us do right in your eyes. For thine is the Kingdom, the Power and the Glory. In Jesus' mighty name we pray... THANK GOD...

Amen.

NOTES

Week Nine

1. A Never-Failing God

Isaiah 43:18-19:

"Do not remember the former things, nor consider the things of old. Behold, I will do a new thing. Now it shall spring forth; shall you know it? I will make a road in the wilderness, and rivers in the desert."

Heavenly Father, we thank you and praise you for bringing us to a brand new week. No one else could have done it, only you, Lord Jesus. Search our hearts today, Father God, remove anything that stands in the way of our faith in, and love for you. Give us your strength and peace today, Lord. Grant us wisdom, knowledge and understanding to handle every situation we face today and throughout this week. Father, thank you for doing exceedingly, abundantly above all we could ask, think or imagine. Thank you for giving us your best. We ask today that you break every yoke over our lives and families. Let us experience new beginnings, new breakthroughs, new hopes and aspirations, and new visions for greatness in our lives this week. Let your will be done as we move forward in our lives. Deliver us from our enemies, because in you we take shelter. Teach us to do your will, for you are our God. In Jesus' mighty name we pray... THANK GOD...

Amen.

NOTES

Heavenly Father, we come to you today with thanks in our hearts and mouths full of praise! We bless you because you are worthy! Thank you for redeeming our lives from the pit of Satan. Thank you for leading us in the way everlasting today. Father, thank you for another week to praise you, and magnify your name. Thank you for all you have done in our lives. Help us to see your hand of blessing in all we do this week as we continually acknowledge and praise your holy name. Holy Spirit, be our guide continually and grant us peace. In Jesus' mighty name we pray... THANK GOD...

Amen.

NOTES

Lord, we love, praise and glorify your name. We praise you for being our shepherd, in which we shall not want of anything. Lord, as you open our eyes to see the sunrise, we are uncertain of what today and the days ahead may bring, but we pray for your divine protection, and have the faith and trust that you will pull us through.

Heavenly Father, thank you for making us strong even in the midst of the storms of life. Today we reject every negative thought and reject lies from the past. We break every stronghold through the power of your word and embrace your truth which sets us free. Thank you for teaching and guiding us and giving us direction in our lives. Father, today we receive your counsel. Help us to be more like you and to hear you clearly. Give us your strength and great peace today and throughout this week, to stay faithful to your holy word. Today we reign over sin, poverty and sickness, and we will live a life that is pleasing to you. In your son Jesus' name... THANK GOD...

Amen.

NOTES

4. A Prayer for the Struggling

Heavenly Father, as we come to you on bended knees, we thank and praise you for another day. Thank you for waking us up this morning, and for strengthening our minds and bodies. We open our hearts to you and receive your perfect peace and love. Fill us with confidence and reassurance, Lord God, as we embrace everything you have for us today.

Lord, we lift up all those who need an extra dose of your power and strength today, those who are dealing with tough decisions, and those who may be struggling with difficult situations beyond their control. Give them strength so that they don't get tired of waiting or doing good, speak clear and loud because you never leave us nor forsake us. Help them to understand that some things take time to change, but progress is being made. We know that in your time, you make all things work for our good. Please show them today as you're teaching them your way, that your timing will be right. Help us to be humble, and have all faith and trust in you. Thank you for ordering our steps and ordaining our future, as we surrender all to you, Lord Jesus. In Jesus' name we pray... THANK GOD...

Amen.

NOTES

The book of Romans tells us that faith comes by hearing the word of God. The more we fill our hearts and minds with God's word, the stronger our faith will be, so we can stand against the powers of darkness.

Prayer:

Almighty Lord God, we thank you for waking us up this morning to greet another day and live for you. Father, we receive your word today, which is life, health, and strength. God, we know that a lot of things can go wrong in our lives today, so we ask that you help us to have faith and trust in you, and choose to focus on you and your goodness. Remind us how much we need you and rely on your presence and your strength to fill us each day that we rise. We pray that you let your presence and your peace surround us in all that we have to face and carry, knowing that you can carry all things much better than we ever could. We ask that you bring us your joy, for it is only you who can paint true smiles on our faces, and it is only you who can bring us joy that is full, complete and lasting. At the end of each day, remind us to thank you for every blessing you have given us. Thank you that through our every weakness, it is your strength that is displayed in our lives. It is your strength that we will forever stand in. For thine is the Kingdom, the power and the glory... THANK GOD...

Amen.

NOTES

Week Ten

1. On Christ the Solid Rock We Stand, All Other Ground is Sinking Sand

Heavenly Father, today we believe that you have our miracles in the palm of your hand. We know that nothing is too hard for you. We trust in your word as you said in Luke 15:31: "You are always with us and all that I have is Yours."

Father, thank you for being with us even in the hard times. We praise you today because you are faithful, and we know you are always leading and guiding our steps. Help us to keep our mind focused on you, and keep us in perfect peace. Help us to be more mindful of others, to be giving, loving, kind, gracious, thankful, and patient with people. Help us to be a reflection of your love, your goodness, grace and mercy. Thank you for every blessing and trial because they make us strong. We give you praise and all the blessings, and honour you today. We thank you for your goodness in our lives. Thank you for filling us with your strength and joy as we praise and worship you today. In Jesus' mighty name we pray... THANK GOD...

Amen.

NOTES

2. Thank You for Being with Us Today

Lord, we thank you for another day. Thank you for being everything that we need, just when we need it. We thank you for supplying everything we need according to your riches in glory.

Heavenly Father, today we believe that you have our miracles in the palm of your hand. We know that there is nothing too hard for you. Help us to stand strong in faith and keep us close to you. Father, thank you for being with us, even in the hard times. We praise you today because you are faithful, and we know you are always leading and guiding our steps. We bless you today, and we thank you for your goodness in our lives. Thank you for filling us with your strength and joy as we praise and worship you today and throughout this week. We surrender everything totally and completely to you. We give you praise, glory and honour for the victory. Satan, you're defeated – you have no place, power or authority in our lives. In Jesus' mighty name we pray... THANK GOD...

Amen.

NOTES

2nd Corinthians 5:7:

"For we walk by faith, not by sight."

Lord, we thank you for speaking to us and showing us the way to go. You gave us so many examples in your book of how we should use your word, and we know that you will bring us through. We thank you that you will continue to walk with us. Heavenly Father, as we start this new day, we ask you to put the joy of living back into our hearts. Give us back what the devil has stolen from us, and let us rejoice, trust, and have faith in your restoration.

You remind us daily we should not fear because the battle is yours, Lord, not ours. Help us today to encourage each other, so that our faith will not rest on human wisdom, but on your power to control all things. Lord, we continue to pray for protection for our families and friends. Cover them with your strength, so they may persevere in times of trial, and give them the faith to stand strong on your word. Renew our minds to your word that we may submit to your truth, and declare that we are strong in you. We have enough evidence that you, Almighty Father, run this earth, no one is greater than you. You are our God, and King, in your mighty name we do pray and declare... THANK GOD...

Amen.

NOTES

Dear Lord Jesus, we thank you for blessing us this morning. We place today into your hands. Lead us not into temptation, give us the strength and grace to keep our hearts pure and guarded against all the things that are not right in our life. We trust and seek you, and put you first; you will direct our steps.

Heavenly Father, today we set our hearts and minds on you, knowing that you are good and faithful. Today we choose to remain in you and follow your lead in everything we do. We give you all that we are and keep our eyes on you. God, we declare today that we are free from every plan of the enemy. Thank you for sustaining us and empowering us to fulfil your call on our lives. In Jesus' mighty name we pray... THANK GOD...

Amen.

NOTES

Merciful Father, we come to you this morning, giving you all the glory for all that you have, for waking us up this morning and for taking us through another week. Thank you for the grace of being alive and for the gift of a new beginning. Today, bless everyone in all areas of their lives where they need it most, help us to let go of the past, and all the bitterness that is consuming our soul, so you can open doors for your Holy Spirit to move through us and fulfil all our daily needs. Bring back the hope and love we have lost.

Heavenly Father, today we submit our tongue to you and commit to use it for good and not for evil. Help us to walk and live in a spirit of unity as you commanded. We ask for an increase of your power and ability in our lives so that we can live to honour you. May your son Jesus be at the centre of our homes throughout all difficult times, and may we be grateful for the beautiful gift of family. In your son Jesus' name... THANK GOD...

Amen.

NOTES

Week Eleven

1. God as Our Shield

Heavenly Father, thank you for empowering us to live by your grace. Help us to discern what you have for us and let go of anything that isn't your best for our lives. We love you and honour you in all that we do today. Father, we thank you today for being our shield. You are the defensive wall against our enemies. We thank you for your protection. We ask you for your presence in our lives and our homes, and we ask for your divine intervention; may we replace fear with faith. Lord, today we choose to be anxious for nothing, we choose to set aside our worries and concerns. In Jesus' mighty name we pray... THANK GOD...

Amen.

NOTES

2. You Are the Source of Our Strength

Heavenly and most Gracious Father, we lift our hand to you this morning, giving you all the thanks, praise, and honour. Father, we enter into your gates with thanks, and into your courts with praise. Father, we don't take for granted what you have done for us in our lives. We don't take for granted that you are mighty; Satan would love to take your place, but you are worthy of the praise and honour.

Heavenly Father, what an awesome privilege it is to come before your throne of grace and worship you. Thank you for refreshing us with your word, which is the truth that sets us free. Today we choose to seek you first. We trust your word and follow your lead so we can be planted and strong in you. Father, thank you for sending your son, Jesus so we can live forever and join the heavenly hosts. Today we call on the name of the Lord, we receive Jesus as our Lord and saviour. Come into our hearts and make us new. Lord, bring unexpected blessings into our lives that will meet all our needs, and restore the joy of salvation because the battle will become our victory. In Jesus' mighty name we pray... THANK GOD...

Amen.

NOTES

3. God, We Are Nothing Without You

Lord, you are the chief cornerstone of our life. Thank you for the courage, strength and grace to handle every challenge and difficulty. You are great, you do miracles and there is no one else like you. We pray that you lead us and show us the way we should walk. As we begin our day, let your Holy Spirit be with us, and may it break every chain that is holding us back. Take the lead, be a lamp at our feet, and show us the way we should go. Keep us from all evil. May opportunities and favour come our way, and may new blessings come to all that are around us, Lord Jesus. Let our lives be beautified to glorify you, and release grace and mercy upon our lives today. We know that all powers are in your hands. Your sheep hear your voice and you know them. In Jesus' mighty name we Pray... THANK GOD...

Amen.

NOTES

Dear Father God, we thank you for waking us to a brand new day. We give you all the praise, honour, and glory. Your mercies are new each and every morning we open our eyes. We pray today will be filled with more blessings, new opportunities, healing, and love. Father, thank you for being with us even in the hard times. We praise you because you are faithful, and we know you are leading and guiding us to victory all the days of our lives. Prepare us for the day ahead of us, take away all our worries, trials, and regrets, and recharge our souls with hope, joy and peace. God, we trust you with our whole hearts today. Help us to stand strong in faith all the days of our lives. Father, we receive your blessing and favour today and ask that you direct our every step. Show us your ways so that we may walk with you today and always. In your son Jesus' name we pray... THANK GOD...

Amen.

NOTES

5. Thank You for Always Loving Us

Heavenly and Righteous Father, thank you for loving us today. We receive your promise today, and we will cast all our cares on you, and we will set our hearts and minds on you, all the days of our lives.

Heavenly Father, today we choose to magnify and exalt you. You are faithful and good. We declare that we are a "no lack" people and receive every blessing you have prepared for us. We know that you will make all things work for our good; you are intentional and a never-failing God.

Lord, we so desperately need you to do your will in our lives, and we pray that you keep us forever surrounded with your presence, anchored by your divine guidance according to your will and your ways, and do all that is pleasing to you. We thank you Lord for who you are, and for all that you've done for us in this life. In Jesus' mighty name we pray... THANK GOD...

Amen.

NOTES

Week Twelve

1. Doing Something New

Galatians 6:9:

"Let us not be weary in well doing; for in due season we shall reap if we faint not."

Heavenly Father, thank you for this new week, and for taking us through the last seven days. Thank you for the gift that you have given us, and for what you have called us to do. Thank you that we can be our best, knowing that you will take care of the rest. Lord, we know our time on this earth is limited; help us to live a life that is pleasing to you, and be grateful for every day we open our eyes to praise and worship you.

We lift our hands to you today and pray that you do something new in our lives this week. We ask that you rain on us fresh hope, expectation and peace. Be our shield when we are weak, be our light when we cannot see, be our voice when we cannot speak. Lead us to the path you choose for us, whilst we are still here. We pray that you continue to make a way in our lives, so we will make a difference to others. In your name, Jesus... THANK GOD...

Amen.

NOTES

2. Surrendering to God

Heavenly Father, we come before you today, because you're good and your mercies are new each day. Father, we know you are a sovereign and mighty God, and all power is in your hands. We know you are a God that cares, and we place every situation that we face today into your care. We surrender everything to you, dear God. Whatever is hindering us, we ask that you remove it, Lord. Release your grace, mercy and power from Heaven today. Give each of us your strength and energy to follow you, and the courage to change our life for the better. Make us strong enough to face our fears, Lord, and bless us so that we may never surrender to whatever challenges come our way. Help us remember not to just call upon you when there are dark moments in our lives, but to bow to you always in gratitude for your goodness and your blessings, which are boundless whether in good or bad times. We give you all the praise, honour, and glory, because it's already yours. In Jesus' mighty name we pray... THANK GOD...

Amen.

NOTES

Father, in the name of Jesus, we thank you for today. We choose to put you first in everything that we do because you are worthy of our praise and thanksgiving. God, without you we are nothing. All we are, have and are able to do is because of your love, grace and mercy. Therefore, we choose to set the tone for our day by starting it with you. Draw us close to you and empower us by your Holy Spirit to fulfil the dreams and destiny you have placed within us. Father, thank you for filling our hearts and minds with the faith to believe that we can do all things through Christ Jesus. We are more than conquerors, no matter the storms we face in our lives. You are good, and you are a rewarder, therefore, we put our trust in you, knowing you have blessings in store for us today. We receive it all, and give you the glory. In Jesus' mighty name we pray... THANK GOD...

Amen.

NOTES

_____

_____

_____

_____

_____

4. *Thank You God For the Breath You Breathe in Us Today*

Heavenly Father and Almighty God, on this day, we thank you for the gift of waking us up to another blessed day that you have made! And on this day, God, we ask and pray that you allow each and every one of us to stand in your strength, remaining our life partner in everything that we say and do. Help us to live an upright and peaceful life according to your ways, so that we never step out of that place of faith and trust in you. Give us the strength and wisdom to stand against temptation. Help us recognise and resist distractions in our life so that we may remain focused on you.

Lord, we continue to lift up those who are struggling, and living in fear. We ask that grace, love, and peace will be with them. Help them to understand that no matter how much turmoil is in this world, you are still in control. May your peace, your grace and your mercy sustain each of us as long as we shall live. Thank you, Father God, for hearing and answering this and all prayers. May your Holy Spirit shadow us with your peace. In your holy name, we pray with a humble and grateful heart... THANK GOD...

Amen.

NOTES

Heavenly Father, as we finish out the week, we thank you for taking us through. If it wasn't for you, we wouldn't have made it, and we are forever grateful for your faithfulness. Lord, we lift up all your people to you this morning. There are so many who are hurting today; people who matter, people you love. We ask a special blessing for each and every one, Lord Jesus; we ask that you open new doors for them, encourage their hearts and give them hope today as you meet their needs. Lord, help us to keep away from the distractions, and any negative thought, and help us to focus on your word. Help us to be kind to others in difficult times, as the Holy Spirit continues to lead our way. In Jesus' name we pray... THANK GOD...

Amen.

NOTES

Week Thirteen

1. Feeling the Stress of the World

Lord, we thank you for your protection today. We thank you for covering us, as we rejoice in this day you have made. We pray that your presence will surround us, as we lay our burdens at your feet. May your divine peace be in our minds and hearts. Holy Spirit, we ask that you help us not to worry about the stress of the world that is holding us down. Let us leave everything today at your feet, as you said to cast our care upon you because you care for us. Father, show us your purpose and instruction, and take away any fear and anxiety that you see. Keep us with a clear mind, good health, and the ability to function as a whole so we carry out your will and plan for our lives. Grant us the blessings of travelling mercies, as we step out on our journey, and thank you for reminding us that you are always with us. We shall remain forever grateful to you as our Lord. In Jesus' name we pray... THANK GOD...

Amen.

NOTES

Heavenly Father, we know that you have a wonderful plan and purpose for us this day. Thank you for your goodness and mercy. Thank you for the battles that you fight for us, seen and unseen. We ask for your divine protection today over our families and friends; you know our struggles, and what we are facing. Lord, we know you have a fresh supply of everything we need, physically, spiritually, and emotionally. Help us to trust you more as we seek your face. Shine your light in our hearts and give us the strength to pursue the path you have in store for us. Fill us with your love and help us to focus on eternity. Teach us to do your will, for you are our God and Father. In Jesus' mighty name we pray... THANK GOD...

Amen.

NOTES

3. Looking Back

Father, as we look back over our life at the things that you brought us through, we just want to thank you. We faced losses that we thought would take us down, disappointment that we thought would make us give up, and yet we are still going, still loving and trusting you after all this time. You know what we need, you know where we hurt, you know where all the question marks are, Lord God. Some of us are surviving moment by moment, God, but you are with us in every single one of those moments. Show up strong in our lives. We give your name the praise, glory and honour, because we know you will deliver. We believe your will and you honour your word above your name. So we thank you, Father, for every blessing. In Jesus' name we pray... THANK GOD...

Amen.

NOTES

Lord, you're wonderful, incredible, amazing. Your grace is upon our life, we have to say thank you. Heavenly Father, today we pray for the restoration and healing of the family, and the mending of the hearts that are hurting. We ask that you bring back peace, laughter, security, and health to families that once had them. Bring back the love and hope some of us have lost. May your son Jesus be the centre of our homes today, and throughout these trying times, and may we be grateful for the gift of family, Father. Thank you for the flood of victory that is headed our way. We set our hope and love in you today and look for your goodness in our lives. Make every crooked path straight, and have your way; we surrender, and give it all to you – our hearts, minds and souls. Father, no matter what our circumstances look like, we know you are greater than our circumstances and will fulfil every one of your promises. We give you all the praise, honour and glory. In Jesus' mighty and precious name we pray... THANK GOD...

Amen.

NOTES

Lord Jesus, we love, praise and magnify your name this morning, because this is the day you have made, we will be glad and rejoice in it. Lord, we dedicate every area of our lives to you today. Help us to live a life of integrity and honour, and to seek your face first and foremost. Heavenly Father, you are our rock and fortress, let us not try to walk in the light of our own understanding, and stumble and fall. We put our hands in yours this morning, and we will be led by you all day. Whatever is ahead of us today, Lord God, cut and clear our path, and let your Holy Spirit lead us. You give us the assurance in your word to fear not, because you have us in the palm of your hand. Today we ask that you bind the hand of the enemy that is trying to divide us, and set us free from the spirit of fear. Lord, we know you are taking us through these turbulent times we are living in, for the battle is yours. Help us today to encourage each other so that our faith might not rest on the wisdom of man, but on your power to control all things. Use us today, Lord, as we leave our life in your hands. In Jesus' mighty name we pray... THANK GOD...

Amen.

NOTES

Week Fourteen

1. Prayer for Healing and Provision

Lord, thank you for everything you've done for us, to us and through us. Help us to always remember we are conduits for your goodness, your grace and your mercy. We ask that you flow through us, so we can be a reflection of your goodness in the world around us, so we can draw souls to you, and let your people know that you love and care for us. Even though trials come with life, there's always the victory that is ours. We will lean, trust, depend, and rest on you, Father. We thank you for the strength to stand tall, and knowing that all things work out for our good, because that's what your word says, and that's what we believe in the mighty name of Jesus.

For those that need healing, we speak healing to their body and soul in the name of Jesus. Heal them completely, Father God. We thank you for those who need provision, Father; this is an opportunity for you to show yourself strong. Show up in their lives in a big way, God; deliver, make a way, and open doors that are closed. In Jesus' mighty name we pray... THANK GOD...

Amen.

NOTES

2. Expect Us to Be Joyful

Heavenly Father, we thank, praise, glorify, magnify you. You are wonderful, amazing and merciful, and we surrender ourselves to you, to have your own way in our lives, and to use us for your glory today. Lord God, we thank you for lifting the heavy burden. We thank you for shifting us in the right direction. We thank you that your goodness and mercy shall follow us all the days of our lives. For those who feel they can't do it, your word says we can do all things through Christ that strengthens us. We have power and we stand in authority, and we do it boldly with the joy, peace and love of the Lord. We can do all things, and so God we thank you, because we choose to start with you. In Jesus' name we pray. THANK GOD...

Amen.

NOTES

_____

_____

_____

_____

_____

_____

_____

Heavenly Father, we know that with you today is not just another day, it's a new opportunity, another chance, a new beginning. Father, we thank and praise you for brand new mercies as you take us through this week. Thank you, God, that we have the strength to endure, and there's purpose in our lives. Thank you for opening our eyes and our hearts, and for giving us the desire to know you more. We thank you for every test, trial, mountain and valley because there's purpose in each and every point of it. We thank you for favour, we thank you for blessings, mercy and goodness. We thank you for provisions and healing. God, we thank you for peace that surpasses all understanding; you know just what we need, just when we need you. We know that when we enter your presence with praise, you enter our circumstances with power. Thank you so much for being a good God, in your son Jesus's name... THANK GOD...

Amen.

NOTES

_____

_____

_____

_____

_____

Lord, we thank you for another day, we thank you for your strength, power, and favour. Help us to not walk in fear or anxiety, help us to not own the spirit of rejection. Father, we are yours, we are loved by you; you care for each and every one of us. Help us not to believe the lies when the enemies tell us we are not enough, and we can't do what we've been called to do. YES WE CAN!! And we say yes to you, yes to your will. Father, we surrender to you, so we can live the life you designed for us, not the one the enemy tries to trick us into thinking is ours. For your word says you have been a shelter for us, a strong tower from the enemy. Lord, keep us safe from all hurt, harm and danger, and we give you glory in Jesus' mighty name... THANK GOD...

Amen.

NOTES

Almighty Lord God, we thank you for directing and guiding us as we end another week. We commit our lives, our needs and our plans for this weekend into your powerful hands. Thank you for nourishing our hearts and minds as we put our trust in you each day. Lord, you are our hiding place, and under your wings we always find refuge. Thank you for your love and faithfulness that surrounds us daily, so we will not fear whatever comes against us. Thank you for giving us the power to make changes in our lives. We receive your strength today and choose to speak to the mountain before us. Father, we invite your will to be done in our lives. Have your way in our hearts and let everything we do bring glory to your holy and mighty name, Jesus... THANK GOD...

Amen.

NOTES

_____

_____

_____

_____

_____

_____

Week Fifteen

1. A Day of Surrendering

Heavenly and Holy Father, we thank you for a new week. We thank you for protecting us and fighting our battles. Thank you for lifting us out of our difficulties and helping us to stand on solid ground. Today we stand strong in faith knowing that you are fighting behind the scenes on our behalf. Father, today is a day of surrendering it all to you. We surrender all the hurt, pain, and challenges we've been carrying around in our life, because we know we just can't handle it on our own. Father, help us to let go, and let you move and manifest in all the situations. Father, we know in our weaknesses you are strong, and we know you know all the things we need. So we lay all the doubt, worry and stress at your feet today, and we ask that you make it right for us. Heal, deliver, and strengthen us. Thank you for your protection, grace and mercy. We thank you for the people you have placed in our lives to support and bless us. Show us how we can be a blessing to others and always show our gratitude. We know that you are faithful. Help us stay focused on you this week. In Jesus' mighty name we pray... THANK GOD...

Amen.

NOTES

Lord, we thank you and praise you for another day. We thank you because you're good and your mercies endure forever. We just love you so much, Father God. Thank you for being faithful, our protector and our covering, Lord. God, help us and equip us to go out into the world and make a difference. Help us to be your change agent, to change the way people see what they can be, to see themselves through your eyes, because you call us your own.

Thank you for saving, healing, delivering and setting us free. We thank you for lifting us up from the low places, we thank you for our abundant life. Thank you for helping us be more than we were yesterday, thank you for a brighter outlook, thank you for removing what is not like you. We surrender everything to you, take everything that is not like you, and make us more like you. Jesus, help us not to hold grudges in our heart, free us from the things that are holding us down, lift us up to where we are supposed to be in you. In Jesus' name we pray. THANK GOD...

Amen.

NOTES

3. Prayer for Those Who Live in Fear

Most Gracious and Heavenly Father, we thank you, and praise you for another day. Thank you that we are more than conquerors through Christ Jesus who loved us. Thank you, Father, we can do all things through Christ. Thank you, Father, that there's no test we can't overcome. Thank you, Father, we can walk through any issues, any care and concern, and come out victorious.

Heavenly Father, today we pray for those who continue to live in fear and are anxious, confused and hurting. Those who want their lives to be better, and to be free from the fears that are being perpetrated by the deception of the mainstream news media. Give us clarity, Lord Jesus. Even though we may not know whose heart is heavy this morning, you know the situation they're in. They may be tired, discouraged and frustrated, but don't let them give up, Lord God. For we know that you are a faithful God who will set us free, and have many blessings on the way just for us. Help all of us to stay strong in the faith today, as the Holy Spirit continues to lead the way. In Jesus' name we pray... THANK GOD...

Amen.

NOTES

Good morning, my Lord Jesus Christ. We thank you for another day you have made, and we will be glad and rejoice in it. You are our strength and power, Lord, and we have no reason to be fearful. As your word says, "Fear not, for you are with us, be not dismayed for You are our God." Lord, so many of us are living with our hearts filled with fear and continue to be stressed because of all the chaos in the world today. A spirit of doom is continuing to be brought on by the news media. But we are looking beyond what we can see today, Father God, and we ask that you let us see things from a positive perspective. Let us know that you have good plans, plans to end all the chaos and give us hope. You are our source of truth, love and everlasting peace. Draw us closer to you, as the Holy Spirit continues to lead the way. In Jesus' name we pray... THANK GOD...

Amen.

NOTES

5. Nothing Will Be Impossible

Dear Heavenly Father, we thank you for waking us with a renewed and refreshed breath of life to this new day that you have made, and for taking us through another week. Thank you for standing with us, and giving us your strength to stand firm, with patience and supernatural endurance, and to keep pressing forward when we felt we couldn't go on. Thank you for your guardian angels that you placed in our path during our time of need. And Lord, we thank you now and in advance for your daily and powerful presence in our lives. Dear Lord, your heart is always towards us, your eyes are watching over us, our children and our families, and your ears are open to our prayers. Father, thank you for the ability to accomplish your purpose, as we set our face towards you, knowing that with you nothing will be impossible for us this weekend. Lord, we give you all the praise, honour, and glory because it's already yours... THANK GOD...

Amen.

NOTES

Week Sixteen

1. A Fire Inside Our Soul

Lord Jesus, we thank you and we praise you for another week. We thank you for your love, power, strength, grace, and mercy. We call on you right now to bring peace to our hearts and minds. We thank you, Father, for putting a fire down inside our souls, and allowing us to push forward even troubled times. We trust that you are with us, and you are comforting us and restoring our souls. We thank you for being our provider, so we have no reason to stress and worry. We thank you that you will open the door, and make the way just at the right time. We give your name the praise, honour, and the glory. Protect the lost, broken, and hurting, Lord God, and let them feel your love, and power. We lift our eyes to you this day; help us to follow your commands and honour you as you direct our steps each day of this week. Remove anything that may hold us back from all that you have in store for us today. In the mighty name of Jesus, we thank you, God...

Amen.

NOTES

Father, in the mighty name of Jesus, we thank you for raising us up to see another day. Thank you for your word, and all the blessings you have given us. We speak all these promises over our lives today, and we are filled with joy that you have said all these blessings will come upon us and overtake us. We come before you today asking that you change us, mould us and make us into better people, believers and followers of Christ. Help us to take heed of your commandments on a daily basis. Help us live a life that is in line with your will.

Father God, we pray for divine intervention and assistance for each and every one of us spiritually, mentally, emotionally, physically, and financially, knowing that in your own way and in your own time you will supply all our needs. We ask that you manifest your supernatural powers to keep us uplifted throughout this week. Soothe our soul that we may feel your assurance, and fill us with peace, courage and joy, in the midst of all our struggles and hardships. We thank you, Father God, for planting within us a mustard seed of faith, and we thank you for all the blessings, big and small, seen or unseen, that you have bestowed upon us. In your holy and precious name we pray... THANK GOD...

Amen.

NOTES

Father, in the mighty name of Jesus, we praise, bless, and glorify your name. From the rising of the sun, till the going down of the same, your name is worthy to be praised. Thank you, Father for another opportunity to live right, to do right, to love right in your presence. Lord, help us to speak words of love and care to someone today. Father, we cry out to you, thanking you for your goodness and mercy. We invite your presence this day into our homes, schools, places of work and mostly into our hearts. We know you will never leave us nor forsake us, and we choose to focus on you instead of our circumstances. We know that with you all things are possible. Father, thank you for blessing us and calling us according to your purpose. Today we receive your word which is a lamp to our feet, and a light to our path. We will hide your truth in our hearts that we might not sin against you. In the mighty and precious name of your son Jesus... THANK GOD...

Amen.

NOTES

Lord, we thank you, and we praise you for another day. Thank you for calling and loving us. Thank you for keeping us from all hurt, harm and dangers. Help us to always declare that you are our God that will always cover us and keep us safe. God, we have experienced so many things, but we still trust and rest in you; there will be purpose in it, it will make sense later, we don't have to understand every detail, we just have to trust you, so we just say yes!! We keep moving forward and hold on to you and our dreams. Lord God, have your way in our lives, be glorified in our lives, heal us from our wounds and hurt. Lord, we choose to intentionally trust and love you in every situation of our lives. You will provide, you will make ways, you will open doors. Satan, you are defeated, you have no power, no authority over God's children. In God we have everything we need because God will supply our needs, according to His riches in glory. We thank you, God, for being what we need, just when we need it. We give you all the praise, glory and honour. We tell the world that you're good and your mercies endure forever. In Jesus' mighty name... THANK GOD...

Amen.

NOTES

Lord, we take time today to acknowledge your goodness in our lives, for all that you have done for us. Thank you for your endless love for us, for setting us free, and for leading us into everlasting life. Lord, you see all that we are encountering; unimaginable and unfortunate trials and tribulations that bring us rough roads to tread, and high mountains to climb. Lord, we can only ask you to continue to walk with us, keep us lifted with your righteous hand, and please be the strength that we need to cope, with hope, knowing that in your perfect time, and in your perfect way you will bring us through the rough storms of life. Settle our mind, body and soul, and let your will be done in our lives. Father, we need your strength and your help and we ask that you grant us your peace and a stable mind, as you work things out for our highest good. We know we will be victorious if we just have the patience to wait on your promises, that in you we can overcome all things. You will wipe away all tears from our eyes, Lord God. In your mighty and precious name... THANK GOD...

Amen.

NOTES

Week Seventeen

1. Lord, You Are Bigger Than Any Situation

Heavenly Father, we give you thanks and praise for another day. You are marvellous, wonderful, and Father, we need you. Thank you for being our source and supply throughout this year. We declare today that our trust and hope is in you this new week. We rest in you knowing that you have provided everything we need for today and every day. Father, thank you for your strength and your guidance. We are opening our hearts and our ears to hear you, God, where you lead we will follow. We praise, glorify, and magnify you, and we stand in your word. You give us the victory and you cause us to triumph, you are our comforter, you keep us safe from all hurt, harm and dangers, and we thank you, Father God. We will be a vessel for you, we will be witnesses for you, and we will tell the world that you save, heal, and deliver, and you will soon return. In Jesus' mighty name, thank you God... THANK GOD...

Amen.

NOTES

Today, instead of complaining, be thankful that you woke up. For every struggle you have, there is always someone out there who has it worse than you. Let's be thankful for each new day.

Prayer

Good morning Lord, it's a good day; a day you have made and we will be glad and rejoice in it. Father, we woke up and chose you, we serve you intentionally, we seek you, and we find you. We knock and the doors are opened. We asked and we are receiving. Help us to manage our spirit and our fear today, Lord God, and we will make sure that we don't get into the wrong space of being too angry, and too vindictive. We thank you for healing, restoration, provision, deliverance, and salvation. We thank you for being a good God; when we look back on all you have done for us, we know our God is for us. We will rejoice in you always. Thank you for the challenges that comes to make us strong, and come to make us better. We want to be more like you each and every day. Thank you for being our Almighty God whom we can always trust with every part of our life. We give all honour, praise and glory to you. THANK GOD...

Amen.

NOTES

Heavenly Father, we thank you and praise you for another day. Thank you for waking us up and bringing us to the hump of the week. Father we are ready! Ready to hear your voice! Ready to follow you! Ready to be great. We can do all things through Christ who loves us; we can face any test, we can handle any situation, we can walk through and be more than conquerors.

We thank you, Father, for always causing us to triumph, but Lord that means sometimes we will have to be in the battle. Prepare and equip us to fight. We are ready. We won't use our own weapons, we will use yours, because yours are much better than ours. We thank you that we are spiritually, mentally, and physically prepared for any test that comes. We thank you that we will pause and think before we respond today, especially if something is wrong. We will respond your way. We want to be more like you. Save us, deliver us, heal us, equip us to be great. Thank you for using us, Jesus. We bless your name forever more, because we will continue to lift up our eyes to the hill, for whence cometh our help. Our help cometh from you, God, who made Heaven and Earth. All praise to you, Lord because it's already yours. In Jesus' name... THANK GOD...

Amen.

NOTES

One more day, God, you've given us one more day. Thank you for making us new. Help us to embrace and rejoice in all that the day holds, for we trust you with every situation in our life, the lives of our children, and the lives of our family and dear friends. Father, sometimes we might not see a way, but we know you will make one. So today we pray that you keep us strengthened by the might of your power, as we know that your power is made perfect in our weakness. Your grace and mercy is sufficient to do the impossible in our lives, and you are able to abundantly do more than we can ask and think. We love you and bless your holy name today. Father, thank you for choosing us and calling us your own. Help us to fully understand the authority you've given by your son, Jesus. As we live by your word, you will always be our defence, and our God, the rock of our refuge. We receive all you have for us today. In Jesus' mighty name we pray... THANK GOD...

Amen.

NOTES

Heavenly Father, we come to you today with open and humble hearts, giving you thanks for another day and another week. You are our confidence and our great hope, and we know you hear each and every one of our voices each morning. Lord, we know that all things work together for the good of those who love you, those who are called according to your purpose. Lord, hear the prayers of those who are waiting on answers to the difficult situations in their lives. Father, you said you will take the negative circumstances in our lives, and turn them into positives, give us answers to the decisions we need to make, and let your will be done in our lives today. Lord, we don't know what the future holds but you know the beginning and the end of it all, and we leave our lives into your hand. Today, we will rise up and reflect your glory! Let everything we do bring honour to your holy name. Father, help us to keep the right perspective as we go about our day. Help us to declare new things so we can take hold of all that you have prepared for us for the weekend ahead. In Jesus' mighty name we pray. THANK GOD...

Amen.

NOTES

Week Eighteen

1. Faith Is the Key to Everything

Lord, you're good and we thank you. We thank you for waking us up this morning, we thank you for purpose, strength, vision, and destiny. We thank you for the peace that passes all understanding. Heavenly Father, today we lift our eyes off our circumstances and set our focus on you. You tell us in your word that you are the God who is able to meet all our needs, we know you will withhold no good things from those who love you. We thank you for the beginning of another glorious week of your grace and favour in our lives. We know that with you, all things are possible. Show us your ways this week. Show us your love and all of the good things you have prepared for us. We ask for an increase of your favour and blessings on our lives. We believe your word which says you are faithful and your word is forever settled in Heaven. Manifest your power, goodness and mercies on our lives each day of this week. We ask that those who are weary and carrying a heavy burden today replace their anxious thoughts with your peace. Help all of us today to share the love in our hearts, and expect your blessings as the Holy Spirit leads the way. In Jesus' mighty name we pray... THANK GOD...

Amen.

NOTES

2. Our God is Undefeated

Heavenly Father, we give you thanks and praise for another day to lift your name in praise. Lord, today show your hand in our lives, be gracious to us according to your faithful love and abundant compassion. You are a God that makes all things new. We are overcome, Lord God by your blood, because you have given us the victory. Give us restoration in our lives, so all the challenges we are facing we can be healed, and no more chains hold us down.

Satan, we rebuke you this morning in the mighty name of Jesus. Our God is undefeated, and nothing can separate our love for you, sweet Jesus. Father God, increase our faith in you, and remove all our fears, for you told us that you have not given us a spirit of fear, but courage, love and a sound mind. Lord, we know when negative things happen, we can face them with confidence because you are in control. We owe you our life; so many doors you have opened, so many ways you make, so many times you heal us. Let us be humble, and take away all unrighteousness, and help us to walk in a spirit of love, peace, and forgiveness. In Jesus' name we pray... THANK GOD...

Amen.

NOTES

Heavenly Father, thank you for your goodness and faithfulness in our lives. We don't know what is ahead of us today, but through your love, grace and mercy you will carry us through. Lord, as we step out into this day, we ask that your Holy Spirit guide our steps, and bring us back safely. We will tell of your love. We will tell of your good deeds. We choose to glorify you in everything we say and do today.

Heavenly Father, you made Heaven and Earth by your great strength and powerful hands; nothing is too hard for you. Father, strengthen us today, and help us to encourage each other. Protect our families and friends in these chaotic times, physically, mentally and spiritually. Be our strong tower, our shade and resting place. May your grace be sufficient for us and may your goodness and mercies follow us wherever we go today. In Jesus' mighty name we pray...THANK GOD...

Amen.

NOTES

_____

_____

_____

_____

_____

4. You Are the Source of Our Strength

Father, in the mighty name of Jesus, as we come to you this morning, we thank you for the breath that you breathe in us so we can rise up and give you thanks and praise. Lord you know everything, beginning to the end. Lord, Jesus, only you can secure our future, and our tomorrow. Lord we speak the covering of the Blood of Jesus over each and every one of us. We pray that faith reigns in our lives instead of fear, we pray that joy is in our minds instead of sadness, we pray that peace reigns in our hearts and mind instead of worry. Lord, take control of our lives.

Thank you, King Jesus, that you have given us the authority to overcome the enemy. Satan, you have NO authority over our homes, you have no say over our families, our future, or our health. We trust in you, Lord, it is you we give the glory and praise, you are our refuge and chief cornerstone. Protect all of us from everything we cannot see. Restore our soul today, and lead us in the good plan you have for us. In Jesus' mighty name... THANK GOD...

Amen.

NOTES

Lord, we thank you for being in control. We surrender our steering wheel to you, Lord Jesus, because you are in the driver's seat. We are sitting with you, Lord God, you tell us when to go, and we will go! You tell us what to do, and we will do it. With no fear, no reservation, and no anxiety, we say YES to you, Lord Father. We surrender everything to you; have your way today in our lives, use us for your glory. Bless us today, and we will lift you and magnify you; we will tell the world you're good, and your mercies endure forever. Restore our soul today and lead us in the good plan you have for us. Thank you, God, for doing new things in our hearts, for pushing us forward to our destiny, remembering that you will keep us in perfect peace. In Jesus' mighty name we pray... THANK GOD...

Amen.

NOTES

Week Nineteen

1. We Are No Longer Slaves of Fear, Because We Are Children of God

Lord, we just love you so much. Thank you for being with us and waking us up to a brand new day. Father, help us to choose you on purpose, help us to be intentionally kind, help us to start our day with you, help us to always abide in you and to always put you above all others. As your word says, "Draw near to God, and He will draw near to you"... "He is a rewarder of those who diligently seek Him." Guide us today, Father in all truth, and show us the things to come.

Lord, we lift up those who are going through difficult times; stand by them, give them the strength to endure and grow in faith in these trying times. Fill our cup, Lord, and let it overflow with love, joy, and peace. We know you are a good God, with a good plan for our lives, as we humbly wait on you. Thank you for answering our prayers. In Jesus' mighty name... THANK GOD...

Amen.

NOTES

Heavenly Father, you are the one seated forever to reign, you are our sun and shield. You said you will withhold no good thing from those who love you. Today we put our dreams, desires, hopes and longings into your loving hands. We commit all our plans to you, and ask that you give power to our efforts. We trust that the vision you have given us is for an appointed time. We know that your timing is best so we will praise you until we see your promise.

Father God, thank you for being our ever-present help during our troubles and challenges. We trust today that you are with us, and that you are comforting us and restoring our souls. Lord, place a shield of protection around our families, children, grandchildren, and friends. Let no harm come to them in the days ahead. Give them an extra dose of your love and protection, cover them and comfort them. Thank you for answering our prayers, thank you for turning things around, making ways, and opening doors as only you can. Help us to follow your commands and honour you as you direct our steps each day of this week. Father, remove anything that would hold us back from all that you have in store for us today. Be gracious to us and smile on us with your favour, mercy and grace. Let us feel your presence and voice today. In Jesus' mighty name we pray... THANK GOD...

Amen.

NOTES

Lord, we thank you and we praise you for another day. We appreciate the breath that you put in our bodies; we don't take it for granted, Lord Jesus, and we ask that you help us to be a reflection of your love and grace today. Be our strength, joy, and peace, Lord, and we will rest in you, and trust in you in the name of Jesus. You are glorious, marvellous, wonderful, and righteous, and we bless your holy name, because you are the source of our strength. We thank you for everyone under the sound of our voice this day, keep us in the centre of your will and the palm of your hand. We declare we will serve you with our whole hearts all the days of our lives. Help to love others as you love us, give us opportunities to be a blessing everywhere we go. Give us a breakthrough this day; we pray you will send restoration, and favour, in the mighty name of Jesus... THANK GOD...

Amen.

NOTES

_____

_____

_____

_____

_____

Heavenly Father, we thank you for sending your guardian angels to watch over us throughout the night. For those who didn't make it to see the light of the day, may their soul be at peace with you. Thank you for an endless supply of joy; we cast all our cares on you and praise you because you are worthy. Let joy flow through us as we honour you in all we say and do. Father, we just want to thank you for your grace and mercy. We trust that all our days are ordered by you. We ask that you strengthen and empower us to fulfil your call on our lives. We look to you for help. Uplift our hearts and rekindle our faith so that we may think clearly with a calm mind and soul, and always realize that you are a faithful and everlasting God who never fails nor forsakes us, even when our faith is being tested. Thank you for showing us your salvation and deliverance. In Jesus' mighty name we pray... THANK GOD...

Amen.

NOTES

Lord, you're good and your mercies endure forever. We thank you and praise you for another day. We thank you for your power, love, grace and mercy. We thank you for another chance to get it right. We thank you that you will help us to put you first in all that we do. Father, we come today to create a space for you, because we know you are a great guide. Help us to keep our mind stayed on you, for we know you will keep us in perfect peace. Protect our children, our families, and our friends today, cover our homes as we come and go, keep us from all hurt, harm and dangers.

We thank you, Father, for this is a day of victory. We thank you that we are walking in divine victory and glory. Help us to be a witness and a light for you. Help us to shine, and remember we are yours. Give us your grace to hold our peace, so that nothing will steal our joy. We are thankful today and bless you with our faithfulness. In Jesus' mighty name we pray... THANK GOD...

Amen.

NOTES

_____

_____

_____

_____

Week Twenty

1. Shine Your Light Upon Us

Our most gracious, merciful, and wonderful saviour, we thank you for the gift of life, and for allowing us to see another beautiful day. Guide us today on your path of hope, faith, and love. Keep us safe, and embrace us with your love and protection. Lord, if we are lost lead us to the right path; if we stand in darkness shine your light upon us, Lord Jesus. Use us to be a blessing to others everywhere we go. Thank you for every good thing you have done for us, help us to see clearly what your plans are for us. Keep reminding us that it is only you who has the power to get us through all things beyond our control, in the midst of all that we encounter. Lord, you are our rock, our fortress, and strong tower, and we thank you that we can rely on you, in and through all things. In your name, Jesus, we pray, so it is, we let it be. THANK GOD...

Amen.

NOTES

2. Thank You for the Dark Days

Lord, let your glory fill our house this morning, as we lift our hands to praise you. We pray in expectation of the great things you are going to do, Lord God. You are going to show yourself strong in our lives, and if it is not for us, it's for your glory. We thank you, God, for the test, and the trials that come to make us strong. We thank you for even the dark days, that make the bright days even better. Illuminate your purpose in our lives, God, for those who feel like they are in a dark place, who feel like it will never change. Remind them you will do all things well. We will wait patiently, we will not rush, Lord, but wait upon you, and we will give you all the glory while we wait. Have your way in our hearts today, so that we can be a shining light of your love to the people around us. In Jesus' mighty name we pray... THANK GOD...

Amen.

NOTES

Heavenly Father, you are the one and only true God from beginning to the end. You have been with us, you are with us now, and as you told us, you will always be with us. Father, we give you thanks and praise for another day; let it be better than yesterday, so we live more in accordance with your Holy Spirit. Not by might, nor by power, but by your spirit O God, may we learn and teach others of your goodness and mercy. Clothe us in love and kindness, so we are worthy to minister to those who maybe dependent on us, whether they be rich or poor, high or low; may we do what is required to help, to be a blessing as you have blessed us to be.

Help us today to smile, appreciate the minute things in life, and love others as you love them. Fill our cup, Lord, and lift it up, quench the thirst of our soul, and make us whole. In Jesus' mighty name we pray... THANK GOD...

Amen.

NOTES

_____

_____

_____

_____

_____

4. A Loving and Forgiving God

Heavenly Father, thank you for choosing and using us for your glory. Today we rest in the knowledge that our life is in your hands. Father, we are so thankful that we can bow our heads to you in prayer, and even though we may speak low, you hear us. And on this day, God, we ask that you search us and forgive us for anything that we may have said or done that was not right or pleasing to your eyes. God, we know that we all make mistakes, and we know that each rocky road we cross in our life will make us stronger if we have the courage to keep pressing forward. But we are thankful that you are a loving and forgiving God, and know you will work out all things for our good. So Father God, we ask and pray that you help us to do better for ourselves, and more importantly, teach us how to have a better and loving relationship with you so we may increase our inner faith, increase our strength in and through you, and trust you through everything. Thank you for remaining at the forefront of our lives, whether we recognise it or not. Father, help us to keep our eyes and mind on you, no matter the challenges we are currently facing. In your son Jesus' name, we pray... THANK GOD...

Amen.

NOTES

Heavenly Father, thank you for waking us up this morning, for letting us see the light of a brand new day, for starting us on our way; for this we give you thanks and praise. For every mountain you bring us over, for every trial you see us through, we have no other God but you to give thanks and praise. Be with us all day long, cover us and carry us, keep us safe from all hurt, harm and dangers. Thank you, God, for using us to do great things for you, but first, God, do great work on us; you are our hope. Change our minds and our hearts, help us to see things the way that you see things. Help us to believe that all things are possible. Help us to trust you with all our hearts, help us to seek you, help us to knock, because we know the door will be opened. Lord, you gave us this day for a purpose; show us what you want us to do, and who you want us to be. We submit our will to yours, asking that you do your will in us. Help us to remember that you're always right by our side, no matter what. Bless your children, and meet all of their needs as the Holy Spirit continues to lead the way. In Jesus' name we pray... THANK GOD...

Amen.

NOTES

Week Twenty-One

1. Faith Is a Boat That Works in God's Favour

Heavenly Father, we thank you for storing up blessings for us. We give you all the praise, honour and glory for waking us up and taking us to the beginning of another week. We put our faith and hope in you, knowing that you will have the final say in our life, because we have no reason to fear. You are our light and salvation. Anoint us so we can move forward in the path you have for us. Give us the grace to accept your timing, as we ask for your strength to stand strong while we wait for the untold blessings you have in store for us. Lord, we thank you for giving us victory over all things; no matter where we are, we know you are with us, guiding and guarding us, protecting us and keeping us safe from all hurt, harm and danger. Have mercy on our souls, Lord Jesus. Fill us with your love, peace, and grace. We receive your blessings of direction and protection today. In Jesus' mighty name we pray... THANK GOD...

Amen.

NOTES

Heavenly Father, we thank you and praise you for another day. Thank you for your word which is life to our soul. Thank you for challenging and changing us, for moving us towards our destiny, because salvation belongs to us. We have everything, God, because your stripes say we are healed, no matter the pain, hurt, or heartache. Thank you for meeting all our needs, according to your riches in glory. Thank you for removing fear, doubt and anxiety. Thank you for replacing it with peace, love, and joy. Thank you for the favour, grace, and mercy that you place on our lives. We know your hands are not too short for you are able to do great work in our lives today and the rest of this week. In Jesus' name we pray... THANK GOD...

Amen.

NOTES

3. Blessings on This New Day

Dear Lord, we thank you for blessing us to be able to see, hear and move on this new day. Lord, we can do nothing in our own strength and on this day, we ask and pray for your grace and mercy to lead and guide us. Help us to focus on what really matters in our lives: our loved ones, our family and friends, and all those we hold dear. Help us to do right by one another according to your command, making all the wrongs "right". Help us to set aside our differences so that we all can truly live a life of love. Carry us through the ups and downs of life so that we may see the silver lining in every cloud. Grant us the wisdom to say no to all the things that you do not call on us to do, knowing that our peace depends upon you alone. Lord, give us the strength to bear all, assuring us that all will be okay. Keep us forever reminded that the joy of the Lord is our strength, our peace and our hope for all that is ahead of us. So it is, and we let it be. In your name we pray... THANK GOD...

Amen.

NOTES

_____

_____

_____

_____

On this day, Lord, we come before you on bended knees, lifting our hands in prayer for your refreshing over us. Amazing Grace, how sweet the sound, you are the keeper of our soul – make all things new in our hearts, in our minds, and in our lives. Keep our footsteps firm on your solid foundation, and help each of us to be consistent and faithful in understanding and carrying out your will, hearing your voice, knowing your ways, and obeying you in all things. Please give us wisdom and discernment as we journey through life with your Holy Spirit leading the way. Teach us to walk with an awareness and sensitivity to you every moment of every day. Let your will be done in our lives, Lord. Where you see that we are weak, make us strong. May we all find strength through knowing that it is you who holds us, and keep us lifted with your righteous hand, for you are the only place where we can find peace and strength. Thank you, Lord, for taking care of each and every one of us in the very best way, according to your will and master plan. You are our Father, and we thank you for being the Lord of our life every day. THANK GOD...

Amen.

NOTES

5. Lord, You Are Crucial to Us All

Heavenly and Mighty Father, we lift our voice this morning thanking you for brand new mercies. All things are possible with you, Lord Jesus, and for this we give you all the praise, honour, and glory. Pour upon us your grace and love as we bow at your feet. Bestow upon us the grace that will prepare us for whatever you have in your plan for us today, and the weekend ahead. Lord, as we continue to pray for all who are still struggling, and living in fear, we ask that grace, love, and peace which comes from you will be with them. Help us to remember that no matter how much turmoil the world is in, you are still in control. May your Holy Spirit fill us with hope today, as you continue to lead the way. Help each of us to be a blessing to others today; help us show more love and kindness, and take away selfishness, grudges, and bitterness. Lord Jesus, we give you all the praise... THANK GOD...

Amen.

NOTES

Week Twenty-Two

1. Another Chance to Get It Right

Heavenly Father, we thank you, magnify, glorify and praise you for another day, another chance, another opportunity to give you praise, another chance to get it right, another chance to love, and help somebody, another chance to be better, to deal with our own brokenness and be honest about it. We surrender all to you, because we know there's a purpose for us, Lord. Every day you give us new opportunities, Father, your goodness and mercy shall follow us all the days of our lives. Help us today to stay focused on you. Thank you for guiding and guarding our every step. Open doors that are closed, and make every crooked path straight. Thank you for restoring life, peace, health, and wholeness to our mind and bodies. Help us not to be dismayed and discouraged, but rather be grateful that we are not where we used to be. And Father God, no matter what life throws at us, we pray that you will give us the strength to finish strong, and let your grace and mercy overshadow us with no bounds today and beyond. In your name, Jesus, we pray... THANK GOD...

Amen.

NOTES

2. God Is in Control

Father God, we thank you for waking us to another day of sunrise with a renewed and refreshed breath of life. Knowing that we are not perfect people living in a perfect world, we ask that you sustain and keep each of us in your will and allow us to surrender to you anything that is unlike you. Where there is hatred, teach and show us your love; where there is madness, fill us with your peace; where there is sorrow, give us your support and comfort; and where there is sadness, fill us with your joy and happiness. Lord, even in turmoil you are in control, even when people are angry, nervous, afraid and in tears you are in control. You are our keeper, our sovereign Father, and we give you all the praise. Teach us how to cope with the worry, doubt, fear, insecurities and uncertainties that we may encounter in our daily life. We ask that you order our steps and guide us through rough patches, stumbling blocks and barriers, and help us to find your way if we seem lost. Let your precious light shine in and through us so that everyone can see that you are the all-powerful God who is directing our ways. We thank you, Father God, for being beside us every step of the way on our journey through this precious life that we are so blessed to have... THANK GOD...

Amen.

NOTES

Dear God, thank you for waking us up with the breath of life. Thank you for strengthening our minds and our bodies so we may win, fight, love, live, overcome, and be more than we were yesterday. We thank you for what you've done, and wait in anticipation for what you're going to do. Teach us to stand strong in you, to choose only your ways, and to walk in your truth. We give you honour, we give you glory. Help us to reflect on your goodness today. Help us to share your love today, help us to be a reflection of who you are in our lives. Help us to control our thoughts and our actions, and the words we utter so we might do what is good and acceptable in your sight. We give you glory, honour, and praise, because it's already yours, in Jesus' mighty name we pray... THANK GOD...

Amen.

NOTES

_____

_____

_____

_____

_____

4. We Need You, Father

Heavenly Father, today we lift up our hearts to you in praise, for there's power in your name. You are our confidant, our redeemer, and there's no one greater than you. We worship, magnify, adore, and glorify your name. Lord, we need you, we can't make it without you by our side, and we know it won't be over until you say it's over. Lead the way, rescue our hearts and come into our lives; we want more of your presence, spirit, love and mercy. Fill us with your faith and the patience to press through every challenge we face today. Load us with your daily blessings and benefits, Lord Jesus, as we put you first in everything we do. We praise you for all your goodness and mercy that will follow us. In Jesus' mighty name we praise... THANK GOD...

Amen.

NOTES

5. *Worry About Nothing, But Pray About Everything*

Heavenly and Righteous Father, we commit to you this morning with thanks in our hearts, and mouths to praise you. Lord our God, how great you are above all the earth. You said that by prayer, supplication and thanksgiving we must make our request to you, so today mighty God, we pray for strength as we go through this day. We pray you cover and keep us safe in the centre of your will and the palm of your hand. We pray for the leaders of every country; give them wisdom in every decision they make, in the mighty name of Jesus. We pray your children will have a heart and mind to live right, to do right. We pray for continued blessings over our homes and families. We bless you because you are worthy. Help us not to be discouraged or dismayed, but rather to be grateful that we are not where we used to be. Thank you for giving us another chance, no matter what life throws at us. Let your grace and mercy overshadow us with no bounds today and beyond. Father, we bless your name, and we give you thanks for thine is the kingdom, the power and the glory... THANK GOD...

Amen

NOTES

Week Twenty-Three

1. Lord God Is Our Strength and Might

Lord, we thank you for a fresh week of hope, love, and mercy. Help us to give all this freshness to others, and reflect you through our hearts, words and actions. Renew our hearts, minds, and lives for the week ahead. Lord, today we place our lives and the lives of our loved ones into your hands, and we pray that you allow each of us to go into this new week with your strength under your wings of love and protection. Give us the strength to get past negativity, and help each of us where you see the need. We know you are able, that's why we put our hope and trust in you, no one else, Lord.

Those who are lost and gone astray, we ask and pray that you illuminate their path and be a lamp under their feet. Make our crooked path straight, and help us find direction and guidance. We pray that we are blessed with your healing hands, God, keeping us in good health to have a beautiful future. Show us ways to reach out and be successful, so that we might rise higher together as we pursue our dreams and ambitions. Fill us with your peace and hope today as we give you thanks and praise. In Jesus' mighty name we pray... THANK GOD...

Amen.

NOTES

Gracious Father, and all-powerful God, we thank you for focus, victory, and discipline. We understand who we are in you, and we can do all things through Christ; not our own strength, and definitely not through our fear, but through your love, Jesus. We can overcome whatever happened yesterday because you give us a brand new day, and we will spread your love and joy everywhere we go. Fill our homes with love and peace as well, Jesus; let your Holy Spirit walk from room to room, and remove the scent of darkness. Let your light shine upon us and deliver us from any path of destruction.

Thank you that we're living with purpose, and that you made us great; there's greatness inside each and every one of us. Help us to live to our fullest potential. Help us to not be afraid of anything or anyone knowing that you are by our side. We give you all the praise, honour and glory, because you're good and your mercies endure forever... THANK GOD...

Amen.

NOTES

Heavenly Father, with your grace and mercy we are at the middle of another week. We come before you today with acknowledgement, knowing that all good things come from you. Keep your hands upon us, Lord, to guide us in the right direction. As we bow down on our knees this morning, we are laying all our burdens at your feet, Lord. Uphold us with your right hand today, bind up the broken-hearted, and take all our burdens away. Give us your divine strength and fill us with the courage needed to face all that we may encounter. Surround us with your Holy Spirit and presence as we rise to start our going and coming. Father, remove all that is not good so that we will make room to receive all the goodness you have planned. May our life be filled with victory, knowing that we will find assurance and satisfaction in and through you alone. Thank you, Father God for hearing and answering our prayers... THANK GOD...

Amen.

NOTES

_____

_____

_____

_____

_____

Lord, we thank you and praise you for another day to see our loved ones and families. God, you woke us up this morning because you have a plan and a purpose for us and our life. Thank you that we can trust you because your plan for us is better than ours. We won't have fear, anxiety or reservation. We will move forward giving you glory, we will keep our eyes stayed on you and you will keep us in perfect peace. Our lives are here to give you glory; help us to remember that in each situation that we face. We do what we do unto the Lord, not for people to see us, know us or recognize us. It is by your grace that we move forward one step at a time as we walk in obedience to your command with you by our side. May your spirit keep us balanced with a calm and peaceful heart. In Jesus' mighty name...THANK GOD....

Amen.

NOTES

_____

_____

_____

_____

_____

Father, we thank you and praise you for taking us through another week. We know that we wouldn't have made it through without you. Lord, today break every chain that is holding us down; break away doubt, fear, and anxiety from us, Father God, because you know and see all that is needed in our lives. As we rise to this new day, please surround us with your Holy Spirit to lead and guide us in everything. Help us to reflect on your peace and hope for a world that so desperately needs your presence and healing. We know we are in the master's hand, it's just for us to keep the faith, trust you, and claim the victory.

Lord, give us your wisdom so that we may learn to block anything or anyone from causing a negative impact upon our personal life. Shelter us from evil and the ill-will of the enemy. Help us to pray for our enemies, Lord, bring them your thoughts so they will recognise all goodness that comes from you. Fill our hearts and our minds with good things, remove hate, bitterness, grudges, and envy, and help us to live the life you've called us to. We know that you are our good Father, with good plans for our lives. Fill us with your peace and patience through this day and weekend as we humbly wait on you. In Jesus's name we pray... THANK GOD...

Amen.

NOTES

_____

_____

_____

Week Twenty-Four

1. If God Is for Us, Who Can Be Against Us?

Thank You Father, Son, Spirit, Holy One, and Saviour, you have given so much. We can't give enough but to say thank you for waking us up to see a brand new day, and the beginning of another week. Father, we lift our hands to worship and praise you this morning because you are a God of love and compassion, there's no one like you. We know the devil wants to be like you, but no one can compare to you and the love you showed for us when you died on the cross for us, Lord Jesus. Saviour, what an awesome, wonderful God you are. Let your Holy Spirit walk through our lives and our homes this morning, meet our every need, heal us mentally, physically, emotionally, spiritually and financially. Fill our hearts with hope, this Monday morning; you said hope makes us not ashamed, because your love is shed abroad in our hearts. Lord God, you have given your son Jesus, the most amazing gift to man, and the blessed hope of all who believe. For this we shall remain forever grateful... THANK GOD...

Amen.

NOTES

God, we thank you for being in control. Shower down your blessings and mercy upon us this morning as we come to create space for you. We lift our hands in praise and worship your name, Jesus. There's no one greater than you. Even through the valleys and the shadows of darkness we will fear no evil, for you are with us, mighty God. We cast all our cares on you, because you are our rock and our shield. Help us to bring all our worries, fears, and anxiety this morning to calvary.

Father, we pray for all those who are grieving; help them to find comfort in you. We pray for our government, not only in this country but around the world, give them the divine wisdom to lead us right; we know that there's no greater governor but you, King Jesus, and we give you all the praise and honour. We pray for our children as they step out to schools, university, or work. Keep them covered into your arms, send your angels of protection to surround them, Father God. Help us to worry about nothing but pray about everything, because you are our light and salvation, we will not live in fear, but will put our hope and trust in you. Commit your way into our lives today and the rest of this week, so that we will walk and trust no one else but you. You know the best in each and every one of us, and you see us for who we are. In Jesus' mighty name...THANK GOD...

Amen.

NOTES

3. Unexpected Blessings

Gracious Father, we lift our hands to give you glory, for you never fail. You are the same yesterday, today, and tomorrow; a miracle worker, promise keeper, our deliverer. Faithful, unchanging God, you are more than enough for us. Thank you for this day, for keeping us in the centre of your will, and the palm of your hand. We thank you for every blessing and trial. We thank you for equipping us and preparing us for greatness, the greatness that is on the inside of us; we will align, and assign our faith to your word. Your word says we have the victory, your word says we are healed, your word says we are delivered, your word says we are righteous and royal in your eyes, and God, we thank you for making us fearfully and wonderfully in your image. Help us to always remember that no matter what we've done, we can leave it at your feet, and you will wash us and cleanse us and make us new. Make us new, Father God, better than we were yesterday, ready for the victory today, ready for the promise that is to come. In Jesus' mighty name we pray... THANK GOD...

Amen.

NOTES

Heavenly Father, thank you for the grace of being alive to see this morning. Thank you for your angels of protection who covered us throughout the night, so we may rise this morning to have the chance to make a new beginning. Lord, we know nothing we ask of you is impossible, that's how we know you are our good, good Father. You are bigger than all our problems, and you have brought us this far not to give up, for we know your victory is coming. Thank you, Father, for your faithfulness towards us, even at times we are unfaithful. Thank you for raising a standard against the enemies of our lives. Thank you for being our God who never slumbers nor sleeps. Thank you for the blood of Jesus who speaks better things over our lives and families; without your grace and mercy we wouldn't have made it to this day. Thank you for keeping us safe, thank you for giving us the strength and courage to keep holding on to you, even when life continues to test us severely. Thank you for healing our minds, bodies and spirits. We declare today there's none like you; in Jesus' mighty name we pray... THANK GOD...

Amen.

NOTES

God, we praise you for waking us up this morning, we praise you for your endless love towards us. We thank you that your goodness and mercy shall follow us all the days of our lives. We thank you, Father, that we woke up with brand new mercies this morning, so despite what the enemy tries to do, we will stay in the fight, we will hold on to you. God, we will trust and believe that there is purpose in our pain; even in this chaotic world we are living in, you will still give us the victory. We know that in the end every knee shall bow, and every tongue will confess that Jesus Christ is Lord. You are our champion, the Kings of Kings, and Lord of Lords. We thank you, Father God for helping us surrender our disappointment, pain, brokenness and even our sadness to you, God, so you may replace it with all that you have for us. We speak healing over our life, we speak peace to those who are in turmoil, we speak victory to end the fight, and we speak liberty to all those who feel bound and feel helpless. Give us your freedom so we may serve you, trust you. We love you and we will follow you, God, help us to be more like you every day. In Jesus' name we pray... THANK GOD...

Amen.

NOTES

Week Twenty-Five

1. *Prayer for a New Week*

Heavenly Father, we give you praise and thanks for another glorious day and week ahead. Father, we thankfully lay before you all we are going through – accomplishments, challenges, difficulties and encounters. We know that all things will work for our good according to your purpose for our lives. God, we ask for divine empowerment this day and throughout the week – spiritual, physical, financial, mental and emotional. Let your Holy Spirit align our thoughts with your thoughts and our actions with your word. Let those things that we've been patiently waiting on you for begin to manifest in our lives today. Fill us with your grace and may we all learn day by day to cast all our cares upon you, knowing that we are all bound for your kingdom, Father God. We thank you for your compassion, your strength and mercy. For thine is the kingdom, the power and the glory, THANK GOD...

Amen.

NOTES

God, we thank you, praise, magnify, love, glorify, honour and adore you. Thank you for strength, purpose, destiny, favour, grace and mercy. Thank you for divine abundance and divine healing, God. Your word says you supply our needs according to your riches in glory, so God, we speak what you already said over our lives. We declare it is done, everything we are waiting for, even if it takes a little while; we will be patient and praise you in the process.

We thank you, God, for showing us who we are. We thank you for giving us the strength to be better and do better. Heal our mind and our soul, heal our perspective, help us to see things the way you do, according to your word. Help us to be forgiving, gracious, loving and kind, more like you each and every day. Help us to think of those who are less fortunate; those who don't have what we have, to give, to sow, to share. God, we thank you for helping us to be more like you. Keep us in the centre of your will and the palm of your hand, cover us and keep us safe from all hurt, harm and danger. In Jesus' mighty name we pray... THANK GOD...

Amen.

NOTES

_____

_____

_____

_____

Lord, we thank and praise you for the breath we breathe this morning. Thank you for the light you shine upon us. Thank you for all the blessings, old and new. You are the righteous King, our provider, our reigning champion. We give you all the praise because we made it this far through this year. Your words give us hope, and where there's hope, there's life. We love you, Jesus because you are the great I Am, there's no one like you.

Lord, as we face today, we pray that you keep us with the strength to pray and not to stray, even when we feel like giving up. Help us to remember you are the door and you will make a way. Lead and guide us on the righteous path through all things, keeping us aware that your favour surrounds us. Help us to remember you are our shepherd and we shall not want, because your mercies endure forever. Lord, help us to continue lifting up your name throughout all we are facing. We trust you and lean not on our own understanding; in all our ways we acknowledge you, and we ask that you go before us today and light the way. Lord, we come to you today and lay our burdens down, casting aside every concern and leaving it in your hands. Keep us on the path that you would have us walk as the Holy Spirit continues to lead our way. In Jesus' mighty name we pray... THANK GOD...

Amen.

NOTES

Heavenly and Righteous Father, we thank you so much for this brand new day, and for giving us another chance to live. Lord, we know nothing is impossible for you; replace our anxious thoughts with positive thoughts with your peace, fill our hearts today with love for each other, so we may be a blessing to others. We pray for your blessings on all our families and friends, and anyone who may be going through hard times. Father, give those who are struggling the assurance today that ultimately everything is going to be all right. Let them know you never leave us nor forsake us, you see and you know everything and you are listening to all our prayers. Give them your strength and increase their faith as your Holy Spirit continues to lead. Lord, may this day be filled with positive news, answered prayers and unexpected blessings. In Jesus' name we pray... THANK GOD...

Amen.

NOTES

_____

_____

_____

_____

_____

5. Make A Way, Lord Jesus

Lord Jesus, we love, praise, magnify, and glorify you. Thank you that we are on the wake-up list this morning. Thank you that your goodness and mercy shall follow us all the days of our life. Thank you for the brand new mercies we woke up with. We thank you that today will be a day of healing, victory, overcoming, abundance, answers, solutions, peace and joy. Today we will say yes to you, Lord Jesus. We will lay down our issues, attitude, anger, bitterness, malice, and unforgiveness, because we know it's doing us no good. Lord, we want what you have for us. We thank you that you will supply all our needs, according to your riches in glory – that's everything we need emotionally, physically and spiritually. We thank you, Father that you are enough, we don't have to make our own way because you made the way for us. So we thank you and praise you, we give you glory, honour and praise on this day. Lord, keep us in the centre of your will and the palm of your hand. Keep us safe from all hurt, harm and danger. Protect us, guard us and cover us with your blood. In Jesus' mighty name we pray... THANK GOD...

Amen.

NOTES

Week Twenty-Six

1. Showing Kindness

Heavenly Father, we just want to say thank you for supplying all our needs, and for making ways when it seems there's no way. Thank you, Jesus, for this day. Thank you for your strength, love, grace and mercy, because you're good and your mercies endure forever. We thank you that this day will be a day of victory, a day of overcoming. We will hear you clearly, we will block out the noise and the chaos of this world, and we will keep our mind, eyes and hearts stayed on you.

Help us to remember that sometimes we need to go out of our way to be kind to someone else. Help us do that today, Father God, because there are so many lost and broken people who need you to heal and deliver. We thank you, Father for blessing us to be a blessing to someone else. We praise you, Father, we will overcome our challenges and move past our pain, and will forgive so that peace can reign in our hearts. Turn things around so we will have testimony of your love and goodness. For thine is the Kingdom, the power and the glory... In Jesus' name we pray... THANK GOD...

Amen.

NOTES

2. A Day of Thanksgiving

Gratitude helps us focus on the only one who is able to turn our problems around for His glory and our good.

Father, in the mighty name of Jesus, you are worthy to be praised. From the rising of the sun, to the going down of the same, your name is to be praised. Father, we give ourselves to you, giving you thanks and praise for life, we are the sheep of your pasture as we enter this day with thanks and praise; even in the hardest season we will always have a reason to worship you. Lord, we give thanks for all our families and friends and for the many blessings you have bestowed on us, seen and unseen.

We pray for those who are in need, and those who are lonely; let your presence rain down on them, Father. We know you are our provider and you will supply all our needs, according to your richness in glory. Teach us today and show us what is good for our life. Help us to do justly, to love, to humble ourselves before you, and to seek your will and guidance in life. God, we are grateful for on this day of thanksgiving, may your love enfold us, your peace dwell within us and your joy uplift us. In Jesus' mighty name we pray... THANK GOD...

Amen.

NOTES

Heavenly Father, your name is exalted above all other names this morning. Lord, we love, magnify, and praise you, and we are grateful for all you have done for us; our gratefulness is flowing from our heart. Lord, in this season of gratitude and abundance we give you thanks, because without you we are nothing. We thank you for all you are preparing for us, for opening new doors of opportunity, for bringing the right people into our lives. We are sure of your goodness, Father God, and we live for your promise that goodness and mercy shall follow us all the days of our lives. We thank you for what you are going to do for us tomorrow.

On this day, Lord God, we pray for the needy, the less fortunate, the homeless, the hungry – be with them, God. Bless and provide them with all that is needed in their struggles – food, shelter, finances, and more importantly, place them in the presence of those who are helpful, compassionate and caring to those who lack. May your peace, your grace, and your mercy overflow and sustain each of us as long as we shall live. Keep us safe today and throughout the rest of the week. In Jesus' name we pray... THANK GOD...

Amen.

NOTES

_____

_____

_____

_____

Matthew 11:30:

'For my Yoke is easy and my burden is light.'

Thank you, Father, Lord of Heaven and Earth. We give you praise, honour and glory this morning for giving us life, and the new mercies we see. From the rising of the sun, till the going down the same, your name is worthy to be praised. As we face this day, Lord Jesus, guard our heart towards righteousness, create in us a clean heart and renew a right spirit in us. Fill our heart with love for you and for everyone. Today let us love on our neighbours, our friends, and even our enemies. Let good, helpful and peaceful thoughts flow through our hearts and minds today. Be our shield and guide, and give us your strength and courage to do all that you call us to do, because you are bigger than any situation. Continue to wrap us in your warm embrace, because we are your children, and you know and you see what's best for us. God, we know you will answer our prayers, for this we will continue to pray, and call out your name, King Jesus – all things are possible with you. We love you and magnify your name, we give you all the glory, honour and praise because its already yours... In our Saviour's name, Jesus... THANK GOD...

Amen.

NOTES

Lord, we thank you for waking us to another beautiful day you have made and given us, and we will rejoice and be glad in it. Lord, we praise you because you are our stronghold, rock and fortress; your grace and love is endless. We thank you, Father, because you are faithful and you will equip us with all that we need today and throughout this weekend. You know what our limitations and our abilities are, and you know where we fall short. Father, through the power of your Holy Spirit, give us the strength we need to face this day. We praise you for your amazing grace that always sees our need and always makes a way. May our faith in you be strengthened daily so that we are able to withstand any temptation that comes our way this weekend. We praise you because you do all things well, and you are the one who sees and knows everything. We ask that you look down from your heavenly throne and bless our day, our families, our children, our friends and even our enemies who persecute us without cause. Let your glory fill our house, as we lift our hands to praise you today. We thank you for hearing our prayers. In Jesus' mighty name we pray... THANK GOD...

Amen.

NOTES

_____

_____

_____

Week Twenty-Seven

1. Prevail Over Our Life

Psalms 55:22:

'Give your burdens to the Lord, and he will take care of you.'

You are the Alpha and Omega; we worship you, oh Lord, you are worthy of praise. We give you all the glory and thanks this morning for waking us up to a brand new day and week; we lift your name on high this day. We thank you for your grace so we may excel in all our endeavours this coming week. Father, you assured us that your plans for us all are good, so we wait patiently upon you. We humbly ask you to renew our strength as we wait upon you. Grant us the courage to hold on, no matter the frustrations, pain, anxiety, and doubt we face. We believe our testimonies will be greater than our test, as your timing is perfect. Thank you in advance for our answered prayers. We declare this week to be a week of answered prayers to our deepest requests – our health, our finances, our jobs, our families, our relationships. Be our shield and our guide, and give us your strength and the courage to do all that you call us to do, letting our thoughts, and words be acceptable and pleasing in your sight. We give you thanks, Lord, because you are good and your praise will continually be in our mouth. THANK GOD...

Amen.

NOTES

Heavenly and Righteous Father, we praise, magnify and glorify your name, giving you thanks for waking us up to see a new day. We ask that you give us the wisdom to handle and face any difficulties that may come our way this day and week. Fill our hearts with joy and happiness, and let us keep our eyes stayed on you, as you keep us in perfect peace, trusting that you will make ways and open doors that are closed, and you will supply everything that we need today. We will bind the enemy in the mighty name of Jesus, and he won't steal our joy today. Father God, walk before us and make every crooked path straight. Help us to walk the path that you would have us walk. Keep us inspired and encouraged, knowing that we will all see brighter days of your peace and joy to come, as the holy spirit continues to lead our way. In Jesus' name we pray... THANK GOD...

Amen.

NOTES

_____

_____

_____

_____

_____

3. Prayer for Our Families

Lord we give you all the honour this morning for waking us up to see, to breathe, and to touch; no one could have done that except you, Father God. Today we ask and pray that you keep each of us with our health, and allow us to stand in your strength, remaining our life partner in everything we do. Father God, we lift up our families this morning in prayer, we ask that you bless, keep and touch all our families around the world. Lord God, touch their minds and souls today in the mighty name of Jesus; bless their children as well, Father God.

We pray that you bring healing and restoration those who are sick, we pray that you bring healing to their mind, soul and body. Father, where there is a devil or attack going on in their lives today, we pray that you will strengthen, and anoint and fill them with your holy spirit. Father, we pray that you break the stronghold of the enemy, we pray that you break every barrier that is holding them down. We ask in the mighty name of Jesus that you uphold all your children around this world. We pray that you will heal the land that we live in, touch our governors, and give them the wisdom to do what is right for us. Heal our families and use us for your grace and righteousness. Father, for everyone who is not comforted, we ask that you comfort them in the mighty name of Jesus. Be our beam of life, and keep us inspired and encouraged. In Jesus' mighty name we pray... THANK GOD...

Amen.

NOTES

Heavenly Father, you are the Kings of Kings and the Lord of Lords. We lift your name above all names this morning, high above the earth, all above every situation, and problem. Thank you for strength, purpose and wisdom. Lord, as we start this new day with you by our side, we ask that you let your holy spirit transform our minds, and help us to follow your example and walk in your ways. We know the road is not easy, Lord, but as we encounter hardships, trials, and tribulations, and all the burdens that weigh down our mind, we can only ask that you lift and remove them, and lead us into your grace, mercy, and peace.

Lord, help us to be kind and think of others. We know you are with us, so we don't have to worry about ourselves, because our life is in your hands. We thank you, Lord for remaining at the centre of our life, in every corner and every avenue, and in the lives of our loved ones, beloved families and dear friends. With a grateful heart we give you all the honour, praise, and glory, because it's already yours. In the mighty name of Jesus... THANK GOD...

Amen.

NOTES

_____

_____

_____

Lord, we thank you and praise you for another day, and for bringing us through the week. Thank you that we have made it so far through this year. We are alive this morning to worship and praise you and let you know that you are an amazing God. You are our strength, wisdom, our joy and our hope. Lord, we thank you for whatever comes next, and we know we don't have to do anything by ourselves. We know you will prepare us for what you have planned, and we know you have great things for us. We will walk today with anticipation, we will hold on to hope, we will be filled with your joy, because your joy is our strength. We give you glory, honour and praise, Father God.

You tell us our greatest need in life is to have a relationship with you, so we ask that you draw us closer to you today, because we know that you are the source of love and everlasting life. Help us today to love as you do and not to do anything out of selfishness, but with humility, and to follow your word as it has the power to heal and transform every area of our lives. In Jesus' mighty name we pray... THANK GOD...

Amen.

NOTES

_____

_____

_____

Week Twenty - Eight

1. He Provides

Matthew 6:26:

'The great provider does what he does best.'

Heavenly Father, we give you thanks and praise for waking us up to a brand new and amazing day; we declare its going to be amazing because you are with us. You have taken us through months of worry, but we are thankful to still have a healthy family, food to eat and a home to live in. We surrender all to you this morning, and declare that nothing formed against us shall prosper. You are our provider, our life is available to you, and we worship you, Father God. Lift each and every one of us this morning, because there is power in unity, and we know you are ready to work out everything in our lives for our good and your glory; we just have to continue to trust and put our faith in you. As we start this new week, we pray that every need in our life is met, and favour and newness will be granted. Lord, help us to remember that greater is he that is in you than anything coming against us in this world. Continue to show us your way, and fill us with your faith and grace. In Jesus' mighty name we pray... THANK GOD...

Amen.

NOTES

Heavenly Father, we thank you for waking us up to this new day, blessing us with a refreshed and renewed breath of life, eyes to see, ears to hear, strength to move our bodies, and most of all a voice to give you thanks and praise. We lift up everyone under the sound of our voice this morning, we pray that you fill their homes with the blessings of the Lord today, and fill our families with peace – your peace that surpasses all understanding. Lord, anyone who's going through anxiety, depression, and fear, we pray that you touch them, and bind the hands of the enemy. Release the spirit of peace over their lives right now in the name of Jesus. Father, sometimes life gets us down, and we find it hard to see all that we have to be thankful for, but today we ask that you teach us to be joyful in spite of what we may be going through. Teach us to pray without ceasing, and to give you thanks and to be content in all our circumstances, without grumble or complaint. Give us your strength, Lord God to bring us through the toughest of times, and fill us with your joy and peace. Thank you for hearing and answering our prayers. In your son Jesus' name... THANK GOD...

Amen.

NOTES

Heavenly Father, we thank you for keeping us and waking us to see and be part of yet another day you have made. We love you, God, for all you have done for us. Your word instructs us to pray for one another, so this day we pray a blessing over each and every one especially those who are going through trials and tribulations in their lives. Father, we ask that you pour your supernatural anointing upon each and every one under the sound of our voice. We ask that you release the divine Holy Spirit of Jesus Christ, that the power of the Holy Ghost will rest upon us all, no matter where we are, and what we are going through. We ask that you anoint each of us, that you will keep us with a mind stayed on you. Father, we asked that you rebuke Satan, rebuke his mind, his plan, and his will in the mighty name of Jesus. We pray that the windows of Heaven will swing open for somebody today, we ask that you just pour out joy, peace, love, kindness and mercy upon each and every one of us today, Father. We love you, we need you, we honour you and we give you all the praise. In Jesus' mighty name we pray... THANK GOD...

Amen.

NOTES

Dear God, thank you for the breath of life to greet this new day. We are blessed and glad to be alive. Lord, give us the strength to face this day because there will be times when we are uncertain as to which path to take, and we are unsure about which way to turn in life. Today we ask you stretch forth your helping hand to lead and guide us on our journey through this life, and allow your guardian angels to protect us along the way. Give us the strength and the courage to keep moving forward for the purpose and plans that you have laid out for us, and please help us to turn away from directions that will cause us to stray, and take our eyes and mind off you. God, you know we are a work in progress, and we are not perfect. Help us to develop patience, and kindness, and speak encouraging and kind words in our homes and outside. Help us to build each other up, not to tear each other down. Help us not to be self-absorbed that we forget to ask how others are doing. Please forgive us when do things our own way, instead of your way. Help us to trust and rely on you to get us through whatever our day may bring. Thank you, Father God, for knowing the best path for our lives. Let your will be done today. In Jesus' mighty name we pray... THANK GOD...

Amen.

NOTES

Heavenly Father, we give you thanks and praise for another day. You are wonderful, loving, and worthy, and you are our God. Lord, we don't have enough words in our mouth to tell you thanks for being our ever-present help in times of trouble. We ask today that you give us our daily bread, because you are our bread of life. We ask and pray that you help us to have a "reset" in our faith, and in our life. Renew our hearts our minds, and our life, for you and your ways. Help us to keep our eyes fixed on you, so we may clearly see all things seen and unseen, and where we should gracefully submit to your will. Father, please let your will be done in our lives, our homes, in our relationship, our jobs, our finances and our families today. We love you, and we will always need you. We thank you with a humble and grateful heart for your promise to be with us, this day and every day of our life. In your name we pray... THANK GOD...

Amen.

NOTES

Week Twenty-Nine

1. Tell Him What You Want, Because God's Love Never Ends

Almighty Father, we give you glory for this day, and we thank you for your mercy and your grace. Thank you for your long suffering towards us. You have never left us, never forsaken us, and because of your great love for us, you remain faithful to your word. You are our refuge and strong tower in every trial and tribulation.

Heavenly Father and great shepherd of our souls, we invite you this day to take full control of our lives. Father, as we kneel, sit, or stand to worship you today we ask that you increase your presence in us and dissolve every pride, doubt, unforgiveness and sins that may hinder the fullness of your power in our lives. Melt the hardness in our hearts, so we will be able to love, because love is you, Father God. We dedicate this week into your hands – revive us again! Reignite that fire, passion and determination to pursue and realise the wonderful dreams and visions you have put within us to fulfil our earthly destinies. Father, revive our careers, businesses, relationships, marriages, finances and most importantly, our love for you. Let this week mark a new beginning on our journey to greatness. Today we will love more, laugh more, and share more with each other. Father God, be glorified in our lives today and every day as ever before. In Jesus' mighty name we pray... THANK GOD...

Amen.

NOTES

Only you are holy, only you are worthy, only you are wonderful, for there's no one else like you. As we rise up this morning to another brand new day, we give you thanks and praise. We are grateful for all you have done. We sing praise, and give you all the glory, hallelujah, thank you, Jesus, we worship your holy name. Lord Jesus, it's because of you that we can experience true joy. We admit it can sometimes feel hard to be joyful in the middle of crisis, but when the cares of our heart are many, your comfort gives us renewed hope and cheer. So today, we choose to take refuge in you; we will sing joy because you are our strength, our light, our salvation. Remind us that we can walk in the fullness of the blessings you have prepared for us.

Lord have mercy upon us, and create a clean heart and renew a right spirit within us to forgive others as you forgave us. Come into our hearts today, O God, and turn our hearts from stone to a heart of flesh. Make us holy and set us apart for your use and glory this week. Almighty God, have your way in our life because you are worthy of all the glory, honour and power. In Jesus' name we pray... THANK GOD...

Amen.

NOTES

3. Believe in the Power of Prayer

Good morning, God. Your word says the Lord is good and His mercies endure forever; we believe in your word, and we thank you for waking us up to a brand new day. Father God, our lives and days are in your hands, because we don't know who or what will cross our path today. Please allow us to anchor ourselves to you and to stand strong in you, and with your strength and courage, to do all we have to do. Help us to remain conscious of all the work you do in our lives daily, and keep us aware of your presence in everything we say and do. Help us to live in peace, and show love to one another for you. God is love, and there's no greater love than you. May the Holy Spirit continue to lead the way. In Jesus' name we pray... THANK GOD...

Amen.

NOTES

Almighty God, we thank you for waking us up to this new day, and we humbly come before you in prayer for ourselves, families, and friends, and all those who are in need. We ask that you keep us encouraged daily, and bless us to fulfil our destiny, the destiny of your choice. We pray that you touch, strengthen and bless our minds today in the mighty name of Jesus. Rebuke the works of the enemy, and we pray that you give us established ways of thinking that are in perfect alignment with your will. Break every addiction, cast down every devil, and remove every hindering spirit in the mighty name of Jesus. Block every tempting spirit that will oppose the work of the Holy Spirit in all our lives today, God. Let your will be accomplished, and as we grow stronger in you, Father God, we ask that you help us to be witnesses to Jesus Christ. Help us to live each day with gratitude, being content with what we have or do not have, and most importantly, take nothing in this life for granted. In Jesus' mighty name we pray... THANK GOD...

Amen.

NOTES

5. Trust in the Unchanging God

Lord, we thank you, praise you, glorify and magnify you. We thank you for your grace and tender mercies that will carry us through today. Please be our shield, keep us safe under your mighty hand, surround us and preserve us from all that are against us. Teach us your way and lead us to a smooth path. Heavenly Father, we know you will not withhold good things from those who love you; you said you will not deny your help to any of your people who ask, and for that we are grateful. There are many people suffering, and going through hard times with no one to help them. Lord, we ask that you meet their needs, and the needs of their families, whether it be financial, physical, emotional, or spiritual. We know you are a loving God who delights in blessing your children. Show favour to those who are in need today. Continue to bless us this year, because some people were promised it, and we know you always keep your word. We thank you for every blessing to come. In Jesus' mighty name we pray... THANK GOD...

Amen.

NOTES

Week Thirty

1. Being God-Dependent

God, we thank you for another day, we love you, God, because your mercies endure forever. We love you, God, because you first love us. We thank you for your sacrifice for us, Father God. Help us to always realise and recognise this. Let your will be done in us today, Lord God, be our light, be our will, be our guide, be our way. When we think of doing things our way, remind us of your great might, and wonderful power, and forgive us for trying to be "self-dependent" instead of "God-dependent." Give us wisdom, and teach us how to live our life according to your purpose, your plan, and your glory. Give us extra strength today, extra love, and an extra boost of your joy, so that we may keep going. Lord, we say yes to you, we surrender to you, and we trust you. We stand on your word, and we believe that great things are to come. Thank you, Lord, for being our defender, and with a humble heart, we thank you for being our Lord every day. In Jesus' mighty name we pray... THANK GOD...

Amen.

NOTES

Heavenly and Righteous Father, we lift our eyes to the hills from where our help comes. Our help comes from you, Father God, who made Heaven and Earth. Lord, we ask that you wash and cleanse us of everything that is not pleasing in your sight; we want you to look at us and smile, so help us to do better and be better. Thank you that today will be a day of victory and overcoming. We thank you that you will walk with us through the rest of this day and week. Satan, you are defeated, and we cancelled every assignment, every trick, every ploy, and every plan that you have set to destroy the people of God; we cancelled it right now in the name of Jesus. Father, speak loud, and where you lead we follow. Open doors that are closed in our lives, and close the ones that need to be closed. Grant each of us your peace and a stable mind with patience and endurance, as you work things out for our highest good. Thank you, God, for first changing us and making us better; help us to spend more time in your word, more time talking to you, more time making sure our lives live up to the way you have called us to live. We give you all the praise, honour, and glory... In Jesus' precious, powerful and holy name... THANK GOD...

Amen.

NOTES

Lord, we thank you for this new day, and for your steadfast and unchanging love. You are faithful, and it is our desire to be full of faith. Help us to stay strong in you; if there are any areas in our lives where we are fearful or full of doubt, we ask that you remove them right now in the mighty name of Jesus. Lord, you sit high on your throne this day, looking down on us, you see all that we are going through. Help us to serve you above ourselves, and to trust you to lead, and guide us as we take bold and courageous steps on our journey through life. Help us to be tolerant, and forgive one another when we have a complaint against someone else. Let us add love that binds everything in unity, because it's your love and peace that calls us together in one body. Please be the rock on which we stand, and give us all that we need to push through these trying times. Bless everyone under the sound of our voice today, God, and plant within us a mustard seed of faith, so we can trust in only you. Thank you for hearing this and answering all our prayers. In Jesus' mighty name we pray... THANK GOD...

Amen.

NOTES

_____

_____

_____

4. God Will Wipe Every Tear from Our Eyes

Father, in the Mighty Name of Jesus, we give you thanks, because your mercies are new each morning. We worship and we magnify your holy and precious name. Lord God, we ask that you release your angels and the anointing of your Holy Spirit to help us realise that you know what makes us cry; you know what is putting pain in our hearts, you know the things that are burdening us, and what is hindering us from fulfilling the things that you want us to fulfil. God Almighty, you know. We pray that you send the angels of your presence to stand by us. Minister to all that call upon the name of Lord Jesus. Draw all of us closer to you today, as the holy spirit continues to lead. In Jesus' mighty name... THANK GOD...

Amen.

NOTES

Heavenly Father, we thank you for everything you have made possible for us so far through this year. Give those who are struggling the assurance today that everything is going to be fine. Let them know that you are right there with them, the one who is always listening to their prayers, the one who can and will turn things around for their good. Remind them that it is always in the darkest hour that you let your power manifest, and pour out blessings on your people for all to see. Today give them strength, hope, and peace as the Holy Spirit continues to lead the way. Father, we pray for divine protection for this coming weekend. Bless, guide and direct our footsteps everywhere we go. In Jesus' name we pray... THANK GOD.

Amen.

NOTES

Week Thirty-One

1. Lord, Let Your Glory Fill the House

Dear Heavenly Father, as we come before you this morning, we thank you for waking us up to the light of another day. We are blessed and glad to be alive. Father, as we rise to the start of this new day, we pray for your divine travelling mercies, and your guardian angels to keep each and every one of us protected in all the ways that we must go. We ask that you guard and keep our minds clear, make us strong and courageous in the presence of all situations, and keep us with a cheerful spirit in all that we encounter, when things do not go as we plan. God, you are our keeper, our provider, and our healer. Heal our minds, bodies and souls in Jesus' mighty name. THANK GOD...

Amen.

NOTES

Heavenly Father, we thank you for your gracious hand that is upon our life. We give you all the glory for all that you have done for us throughout this year, and for what you are going to do for us today. We love you, and trust you in all things knowing that your favour surrounds us like a shield. Today is yours, Lord God; it is yours to be used for your glory. We surrender ourselves, our issues, our cares, our concerns, the good, the bad, and the ugly. Father, it's all given to you. So have your way in us, God, make us better than we were yesterday, fill us with your power, love, grace, and mercy. Wash us and cleanse us of our sins, and whatever we did wrong yesterday, help us to make it right today. Thank you for your unconditional love and care that you bestow upon us daily, and we ask and pray that you do the same for all those that love you, trust you, and believe in you. In Jesus' mighty name we pray... THANK GOD...

Amen.

NOTES

_____

_____

_____

_____

_____

Father, we give you all the glory for another day to see our families and friends. We pray for peace and unity in our families. We ask that you strengthen those who are weak, we pray that you give health to those who are sick in their bodies, in the mighty name of Jesus. Encourage, motivate, empower, and employ your children to go out and do what you said we must do. Lord, we ask that you block the work of the devil, wherever the enemy is working. We pray for all our families, and for those who are going through relationship trouble, financial trouble, chronic sickness, and disease; Lord, please release a wave of your supernatural blessing over their bodies. Lord, those who are worried and stressed out about what the day will bring, we pray that you bring them comfort in the name of Jesus. Release a wave of blessings, joy and your spirit into our lives, and remove the enemy, wherever he's lurking. Thank you for being with us this week and forever more. In Jesus' mighty name we pray... THANK GOD...

Amen.

NOTES

_____

_____

_____

_____

Heavenly Father, we thank you for life, thank you for health, thank you for love, thank you for the privilege to wake up to see another glorious day. This is the day you have made, and we will rejoice and be glad in it. Lord, we lift your name on high, and we ask you to close the door of hate, and open the door of love in our hearts. Deliver us from evil by the blessings your son Jesus Christ brings, and help us to be joyous with a good heart. Thank you, Father, you are with us wherever we go, you have promised to be with us, and have given us your assurance that your presence will accompany us to lead and to guide, to protect and to help. Thank you for being our shepherd, so we may be protected by your gracious hand...THANK GOD...

Amen.

NOTES

Jehovah, in you we trust this morning, you are the God of miracles and all powers, and we give you all the praise and thanks for bring us to the end of the week. Lord, we thank you so much for all that you have done and for all you are still doing in our lives. Father, may we rest in your presence, bathe in your goodness, and celebrate your eternal life. Help us to trust you as our refuge and strength, so that we are not afraid as we rest in your shadow and your ways. Father, we need your strength and your help and we ask that you grant each of us your peace and a stable mind with patience and endurance as you work things out for our highest good. This we ask of you in your precious, powerful and holy name... THANK GOD...

Amen.

NOTES

Week Thirty-Two

1. To God Be the Glory

Heavenly Father, we thank you and magnify your holy and precious name this morning. To God be the glory, great things He has done. We thank you for life; we wake up to see, smell, hear, touch, and this is all because of you, Father God. Renew our minds and our hearts, so we can use everything that you have given us for your glory. Father, thank you for guarding and directing our steps throughout this year so far. Thank you for healing, protection, provision, and peace. Father God, no matter what's going on in our lives, we can always count on you to be there for us. Please continue to help us through challenging times; we know through your strength, mercy, and grace everything will be possible. Heavenly Father, we thank you for placing dreams and desires in our hearts for this coming week. We trust that you are at work to bring them to pass even when we can't see them. May your will be done in our lives today as the Holy Spirit continues to lead our way. In Jesus' mighty name we pray... THANK GOD...

Amen.

NOTES

Father God, we thank you for another beautiful day. Thank you for the opportunity to wake up to see our families, our children, and our friends. We thank you that you are keeping us in the centre of your will and the palm of your hand. Speak loud, Lord Jesus, and we will follow you; hold us close to you, Father God. Help us to remember we are yours, no matter what we see, feel, and experience today; we declare your goodness, we thank you that we will help someone today, we'll be selfless today, and will reach out to someone we haven't spoken to in a long time. We thank you that we will stay positive today, we will focus on the good, we'll speak healing, life, deliverance, abundance, peace, joy – everything that you have for us, God, we want it all. Be our refuge and our strength, and a place of shelter for us today, Lord God, no matter what tries to come against us. We pray that you clear the way in the mighty name of Jesus. THANK GOD...

Amen.

NOTES

_____

_____

_____

_____

_____

Thank you, Jesus, for waking us up this morning. Thank you for bringing us through, for bringing us out, and for bringing us over. We praise and thank you, Father, for what is to come; we expect great things throughout the rest of this year, we expect healing, blessing, provision, strength, wisdom, and open doors, because that's the God you are, the God we praise, the God we serve, and the God we look up to. So we praise you, Lord Jesus, we are conduits for you, you can flow through us; touch us, Father, so we can touch others today. You said that if we ask anything according to your will it will be done, so thank you for your goodness and faithfulness in our lives. Father, keep us closer to you each day of this year, and help us to always follow your words as we surrender every area of our lives to you. In Jesus' mighty name we pray... THANK GOD...

Amen.

NOTES

_____

_____

_____

_____

Heavenly Father, we give you thanks this morning for waking us up today. Thank you for holding our hands and carrying us through, thank you for jumping the broom with us, Lord. We ask that you give us the wisdom to know how to walk the path you lay before us, let this day, and the rest of this year be filled with peace and happiness, as we lead others into your light. Father, we pray for victory over everyone today, we pray that we will come boldly to the throne of grace, and we pray that we will seek your face like never before. Father God, we pray that you will lift up the heavy burden we've been carrying; the heads that are bowed down, lift them up, Lord Jesus. We pray for peace to be in our homes, our hearts and in our midst today, Father God. We declare we will have peace, joy, and love in our hearts. Let no weapon formed against us prosper, and every tongue that rises up against us, we will be able to condemn it in the mighty name of Jesus. Father, we will never forget your goodness, your grace and your mercy that you continuously show us. Thank you for never leaving us. We love you, and we need you, and we commit to walking in obedience to you. In your mighty name, Jesus... THANK GOD...

Amen.

NOTES

Never would we have made it without you, Father God. We give you all the praise, honour, and glory, Lord, you are our light and salvation, whom shall we fear? Father, you go before us and you fight for us; we are not shaken, you cover us, you made your face shine upon us always. Thank you for bringing us to the end of another week, full of your grace, goodness and mercies. As the weekend comes upon us, we choose to face it with you first, and foremost, and in all things that we do and say. Wipe away all the tears from our eyes and bring peace, joy, love and hope into our minds and hearts this weekend. God, we declare that today you will lift our spirit and give us hope as you meet our needs. Lord, we stand on your word that we will fear no evil, for you are with us and nothing is impossible by the power of your hand. In Jesus' mighty name... THANK GOD...

Amen.

NOTES

Week Thirty-Three

1. *Start Your Week with Jesus*

Father, in the name of Jesus, we come to you with a thankful heart and we bless your holy name. Thank you for the new week ahead, and another new beginning. Lord, as we start this new week, go before us and lead us, part any seas that are before us. Thank you, Heavenly Father, for all the battles you've fought for us, thank you for all that you have done, and all that you are going to do for us in our lives. Great is your faithfulness towards us.

Help us in this new week to form friendships that are fruitful, which will help us to be mature in the spirit. We pray that you will help us to walk closer with you and the Spirit, so we will not fulfil the works of the flesh. Help us to walk in your blessings and goodness today, and let your face shine upon us. This new week open the right doors for our lives, and protect us from those we need to walk away from. Let our ways be purposeful, and our footsteps be firm. Give us a heart of wisdom to hear your voice, so we might run this week with your purpose before us. In Jesus' mighty name we pray... THANK GOD...

Amen.

NOTES

Heavenly Father, we give you all the honour this morning for blessing us with another day. This is the day you have made and we will be glad and rejoice in it. We thank you for all the blessings over our lives, thank you for your blood that you shed on the cross for us, the precious Lamb of God. Thank you, Father, that your favour has no end, that it will last for our entire lifetime. Help us not to fear or doubt. We are grateful that you are watching over us, and Lord, keep everyone around us safe and happy. Bless them all with good health, peace in their mind and kindness in their heart. Help us to be the person you want us to be, and help us to honour you in all that we do. Open fresh doors of prosperity to us and lead us to new paths of blessings in the name of Jesus. We refuse death, sickness, accidents, and misfortunes in our lives, and the lives of our families and friends, in Jesus' name. We shall not beg our bread, for you, God, will supply all our needs according to your riches in glory. THANK GOD...

Amen.

NOTES

Father, you are our refuge and strength. We thank you for the first blessings that we receive today – the gift of life. Lord, we come to you for divine protection, we are living under your shadow, your grace, your power and your love. Lord, we lift up the world this morning into our prayers, and into your hands. As the world continues to travel down a dark path, and stress and anxiety continues to grow, so many of us are worried about all that is going on around us. Father, we pray that you increase our faith today, and remove all our fears. Strengthen our mind that when negative things happen around us, we can face them with confidence and courage. Help us to run towards greatness, towards purpose, towards destiny. We release what is left behind, we will expect great things, we will focus on it, we will pray and speak it for your glory. We thank you that your protection and your grace is over our land. We draw the blood of Jesus over our families, our children, our homes, our friends, and we thank you that your angels will take charge over us. We will surrender it all to you, as your Holy Spirit continues to lead. Thank you for your healing, and your grace. In Jesus' mighty name we pray... THANK GOD...

Amen.

NOTES

Father, in the mighty name of Jesus, we thank you for every breath we take. Waking up this morning is such a blessing, and we know as we walk today with you, our life is in good hands. No matter what the enemy tries we will still trust in you. We know by walking with you the enemy has no power, nor authority in our lives. God lift the broken hearted, fill them with your joy and your peace in the name of Jesus. We thank you for the love you continue to show us; help us to show forgiveness to one another, let us not forget the love you showed for us when you died on the cross. We pray that you make our way purposeful and our footsteps firm out of your goodness and love. Give us a heart of wisdom to hear your voice, and make us strong by your huge favour and grace. We declare and decree today our home will be full of love, joy, and peace. In Jesus' mighty name we pray. THANK GOD...

Amen.

NOTES

Heavenly and Righteous Father, we thank you for showering us with your love and protection. Fill us with your joy and your peace. If there are any areas in our lives where we are weak, Lord God, we pray for strength. We pray the power and the presence of your hand overtake us and make us for your will. Have your way in our lives today and the coming weekend, Father God. Go before us and behind us, Lord, and let your goodness and mercy follow us all the days of our lives. Thank you for every victory, and for giving us the strength to lean on you, and not on our own understanding.

Father, you said you will heal the land, based on what we do, and Lord we want to honour your word. We pray for those who govern our nation; may they do it in righteousness, Father God. Lord, draw our hearts closer to you, fill our hearts where there's emptiness, repair what is broken, restore what's been lost. We thank you that we are protected by all of Heaven's angels, and we thank you that you will hear and answer our prayers... THANK GOD...

Amen.

NOTES

_____

_____

_____

Week Thirty-Four

1. When Praise Goes Up, His Presence and Glory Comes Down

Heavenly Father we thank you, magnify, and glorify you. We bless your holy name because you are amazing. We thank you for your amazing grace over our lives, and the lives of our families and friends. Protect us today, Lord God, guide each and every step that we take, lead us in all our ways. We will walk by faith, not by sight, and in your wisdom, and your word. Lord, we know there will be no guarantee that we will live a life free of trials and tribulations, but we know our help comes from you. We trust and believe that you will hear us when we call upon your name. With your grace and favour we can do all things through Christ who strengthens us. We thank you and we praise you, because there's nothing we can do without you. We thank you for the privilege of being able to call you our Father; help us to see your plans for us, help us to stand strong and trust in you in every circumstance. Help us to boldly embrace everything you have in store for us. We love you, and give you all the honour today. In Jesus' mighty name... THANK GOD...

Amen.

NOTES

_____

_____

_____

2. Our Faith Does Not Rest in the Wisdom of Men, but in the Power of God

Heavenly Father, we thank you, glorify, and magnify your precious name. We thank you for protecting us throughout the night and letting us rise to see another amazing day. Your word tells us the greatest need in this life is a close relationship with you. Lord, draw us closer to you, for we know you are the source of our strength, you are the strength of our life; help us today to love you more, and put all our faith and trust in you, not in mankind. Help us today to let go of the wrong things in our life so you can give us the right things. Please give us your grace to keep praising and worshipping you, and to keep the right attitude in every situation. Father, today we call on your healing hands, for all those who are suffering; please heal us all, and cover us with the blood of Jesus. Hear our plea in the mighty name of Jesus. THANK GOD...

Amen.

NOTES

_____

_____

_____

_____

_____

Lord Jesus, we thank you, praise you, magnify and glorify you. Thank you for allowing us to feel your presence this morning. We thank you that our life is in your hands today. Father God, you know our struggles and you know what we are about to face today. We ask that you go before us, cut and clear our path, and steer our life according to your will and your ways.

We lift up our youths into your mighty hand this morning; they are our future, and they are crushed with life's circumstances; help them hold on to the hem of your garment so they can fulfil the promises that you have placed in their hearts. Keep them safe in the centre of your will and the palm of your hand, and make a way for them, Almighty Father. Let your will be done in our life, help us to keep our faith in and through all things, just as you have done and continue to do. We give you all the praise, honour and glory, because it's already yours. In Jesus' mighty name we pray... THANK GOD...

Amen.

NOTES

4. We Have an Anchor That Keeps Our Soul

Heavenly Father, it is always a good feeling waking up to give you thanks and praise. We thank you for your blessings and mercy this morning, and we ask for your guidance and protection. We trust that, with you being our keeper, the sun will not smite us by day nor the moon by night. Father God, send your angels to keep charge over our day, in all that we do, and all that we say. Lord, we declare that no death, no sickness, nor accident or misfortune will come upon us and our families. We cover our lives with your blood. No evil shall befall us, nor shall any plague come near our lives and dwellings. Thank you, Father, that you are with us wherever we go; thank you for being our shepherd – we are under your watchful eyes. Lord, we dedicate our lives to you, we are bound in the mighty name of Jesus... THANK GOD...

Amen.

NOTES

Father, in the name of Jesus, we woke up today with brand new mercies, and a new opportunity to give you all the praise and glory. Thank you for strengthening our minds and bodies. We thank you, Father, that we can do all things through Christ who strengthens us. We thank you for your strength, guidance, and most of all your love. Lord, we lift up those who are going through tough times; help them to know that you want to restore everything that the devil has stolen from their life, and you want to heal every hurt and pain. Let them know you are working on their behalf. Father God, let hope, joy, goodwill, and celebration flood all areas of our lives today, rest this weekend, and set us up to have an awesome week ahead. Give brightness to all those who are discouraged and depressed, let us be anchored where you are, and let your gates be opened today. Father, we just want to thank you that you for hearing our prayers. We give you all the honour, praise and glory. In Jesus' name... THANK GOD...

Amen.

NOTES

_____

_____

_____

_____

1. Nothing Can Separate Us from His Love

Lord, we thank you for another day, we thank you because you're good and your mercies endure forever. Help us to always stay strong in you, in your power and your might. Father, help us and heal us as only you can. We ask that you open up new doors for us and we ask that you lead and guide us through those doors. Show us our purpose today, Lord; show what you want us to do, because we know nothing can stop what you called us to do. Father, keep us humble, help us to remember that no matter how high we get, we are always at the feet of Jesus.

Bless everyone this morning under the sound of our voice, keep us in the centre of your will and the palm of your hand. Answer every prayer, Father, make every way; when you speak we will listen. Remove everything or anyone that is holding us back from all that you have in store for us. In Jesus' mighty name we pray... THANK GOD...

Amen.

NOTES

Heavenly Father, we thank you for waking us to see the light of a brand new day. We are blessed and glad to be alive to glorify, thank you, praise and magnify your name. Father, as we start this new day, we pray that you will walk with us, and let your divine travelling mercies and your guardian angels keep each of us protected, and safe in all the ways that we must go. Father God, you are our ever present help in times of need. We know that we can call out to you, and you will answer. We trust you with all our hearts and lean not on our own understanding but rely fully on you. God, we pray that you will touch, deliver, bless and set all of us free to do your will.

For all those who are looking for a miracle or breakthrough, Father God, we ask that you break the feathers, and cast out the devil in the mighty name of Jesus. God, you told us we will tread upon the lion and the adder, we will trample them under our feet, so we pray today that you will give us the power to drive out the enemy from our lives in the mighty name of Jesus. May the Holy Spirit strengthen and fill us with wisdom and direct our steps today. In Jesus' mighty name we pray... THANK GOD... Amen.

NOTES

_____

_____

_____

3. Prayer for Unity

Father, in the mighty name of Jesus, we thank you, praise, love magnify, glorify, and honour you. How great are you this morning; a loving and mighty God that brings peace so we lean, trust and depend on you. Lord, as we humbly come before you this morning, we ask that you tear the wall down that is causing division amongst us. Transform all the negativity and unpleasant events taking place in this world into something positive, and good for us all. Purify us from all unrighteousness, and give us the strength and clarity of mind to find our purpose in life, so that we may walk the path that you have laid out for us. Let your will be done in our lives, Father God, and let your love surround and protect us from all hurt, harm, and dangers. Please forgive us, and help us to put love over hate, unity over division, and life over death. Be with us, God, answer our prayers, because we are more than conquerors through Jesus Christ who loves us. THANK GOD...

Amen.

NOTES

Heavenly Father, thank you for your faithfulness to us. We give you all the grace, praise, honour, and glory. Father, we thank you for your many blessings, because you are the God of miracles; you are the God of wonders and that's why we believe and trust in you. We thank you for touching and healing everyone this morning, Lord Jesus. You know our trials and tribulations, anguish and pain. We ask that you release divine and supernatural blessings on our lives today. Father, we pray that you strengthen, we pray that you will encourage, and heal and deliver today. Give us the joy of the Lord, and allow us to have the peace of God in our lives. We speak words of faith, and life so that we can partake of the fruit of victory you have in store for us for the rest of this year. In Jesus' mighty name we pray... THANK GOD...

Amen.

NOTES

5. Lord, Lift Up Our Hearts Today

Dear Heavenly Father, we thank you for who you are, we thank you for giving us the opportunity to come to you this morning in prayer. You are the source of our strength, and the strength of our life. Thank you for giving us another chance to live. Remove everything that would hold us back from all you have in store for us. Help us to understand your plans and know the truth of your word that sets us free. We trust that you are with us today, and that you are leading us in the paths of righteousness. Father God, we know we are nothing, and can do nothing without you. Help us to do things right, and to be strong for you. Lord, lift up our hearts today and fill them with peace so that we can lead a quiet and peaceful life in all Godliness and honesty. Our hope must be in you, and our trust must be in you. Father, teach us how to love, because there's no greater love than you. Father, we know you are the Kings of Kings, and Lord of Lords, and we humbly submit to you that your will be done in our lives, in our homes, and in this world. In Jesus' mighty name we pray... THANK GOD...

Amen.

NOTES

Week Thirty-Six

1. Your Mercies Endure Forever

Heavenly Father, you are good and your mercies endure forever. Thank you for this day, thank you for bringing us to the beginning of a brand new week. Heavenly Father, we choose to focus on the good in our lives, we choose to water the right seeds planted in the soils of our lives and minds. Give us your wisdom and your grace as we set our hearts and our minds on you. Lord, we ask that you move and manifest into the lives of everyone. Grant us peace of minds, and calm our troubled hearts. Lord God, we pray that we will experience victory in our lives. We pray that we will overcome any problem, obstacle or any situation. Be our strong tower, provide what we need in the name of Jesus. Father, thank you for a fresh start today; we give you our past, present, and future, and we choose to follow the good plan you have for our lives. Help us to inspire someone and sow seeds of kindness into the hearts of others. Help us to know your ways, Lord, and teach us your paths today. In Jesus' mighty name we pray...THANK GOD...

Amen.

NOTES

2. *In Every Sunrise You Bring Us Hope*

Heavenly Father, we thank you, praise, magnify, and honour you. We thank you for this new day in and with you. Father, you are God alone, and we love you. In every sunrise you bring us hope, and in every sunset you give us peace. We know we are nothing and can do nothing without you. Thank you for showering us with your comfort and love. Pour out your peace in us, and fill us with your joy. Lord, we pray for everyone who is waiting for answers to the difficult situations they're in. We pray that you take all the difficult challenges that we are facing. Give us the solutions that we need, and let your will be done in our lives. Help us to share your love and your goodness as we experience your peace, power and presence throughout the day. May the Holy Spirit strengthen, and guide each and every one of us, as you continue to lead the way. In Jesus' mighty name we pray... THANK GOD...

Amen.

NOTES

_____

_____

_____

_____

_____

Our Lord and Saviour Jesus Christ, we come before you today to thank you for your amazing and endless love. We praise your name today and acknowledge that you alone are our God. Thank you for equipping us with all that we need. We look only to you, Lord Jesus; when we are weak, you are strong. Let your Holy Spirit empower us, and open our minds as you reveal all heavenly things to us. Guide us to walk in the path of righteousness, and free our minds of all constraint and stress. Renew, repair, and revive our heart, mind and soul. We speak peace into every area where there is unrest; we declare your word over our life today. Greater is He that is in me than who is in the world; we know you will supply all our needs according to your richness in glory. Thank you for giving us the strength to overcome the devil; give us the power to walk in victory. We surrender all to in Jesus' name. Thank you for hearing our prayer. THANK GOD...

Amen.

NOTES

_____

_____

_____

_____

_____

4. The Giant in Front of You Is Never Bigger than the God Who Lives in You

Heavenly Father, we bless, love, honour and praise you. Without you we are nothing, without you we shall surely fail. Father God, our lives are in your hands today; help us to walk according to your purpose, and your will. Thank you for your promise of blessings on us, and help us to always be a blessing to others. Father God, there are people who are going through sadness in this present time. Teach us to be strong, and to be there for one another in these difficult times. Help us love others as you do, and teach us not to do anything with selfish motives, or vain conceit. Help us to humbly follow your word for we know it has the power to heal, and transform every area of our lives. In Jesus' mighty name we pray... THANK GOD...

Amen.

NOTES

_____

_____

_____

_____

_____

5. Build Your Hope and Faith on the Firm Foundation of the Son of God

Lord Jesus, we humbly come to your throne of grace today. We give you thanks and praise for waking up to the light of another day. Help us to believe and stand confident in you today, knowing that you are with us, and you never leave us nor forsake us. Lord, give us a spirit of love, power, and a sound mind, so that if the spirit of fear ever attacks us it will be useless. Help us to hold fast to our faith, because we know you can turn the ordinary things into the extraordinary, Lord God. We pray that you move all barriers and stumbling blocks, break all chains in our lives that attempt to hold us back from moving on and pressing forward. We know you will direct our path, and keep us with a cheerful spirit. Father God, keep everyone safe under your wings as we go through the day, and the weekend ahead. Bless everyone with a long and healthy life, peace, love and financial freedom. We declare today that we can do all things through God who strengthens us. Thank you for hearing our prayers. In Jesus' precious name... THANK GOD...

Amen.

NOTES

Week Thirty-Seven

1. All Praise Is for You

Heavenly Father, we thank you for your mercy and your grace that woke us up to another brand new day, and week; another day to be glad and rejoice in. Lord, you're holy, mighty, wonderful, and a sovereign God – all praise is for you this morning, because there's no one like you. We come to you not in need, but with a thankful heart for you are good. We know the greatest need in this life is to have a close relationship with you, and today we ask that you draw us closer to you, for you are the source of all we need.

Father, we pray for direction in all areas of our lives. Teach us to let go of the things that are holding us down, and show us how to hold on to the blessings that we received, so that the enemy will not come in and steal them away from us. We pray that the Holy Spirit continues to walk with us, and that your spirit will help us to live in your power. Open our minds and our understanding; we do not know everything, and when the ways look dim and dark, Father, draw us back to you. Free our mind from worries and cares, because you have not given us the spirit of fear, but of love and sound mind. Thank you, Father, for your presence and for answering our prayers. In Jesus' mighty name we pray... THANK GOD...

Amen.

NOTES

Heavenly and Righteous Father, we give you thanks for another amazing day. We thank you for your power and your work in our lives, and for your goodness and blessings over each and every one of us. Fill the empty places with the truth of your word, Father God. Lord, we lift up all those who need your comfort today; there are so many who are suffering from mental illness, worries about their families, their future, their finances, and their health. In the name of Jesus we ask that you remove all fears, and allow joy, peace and happiness to be in our souls. Father God, do your work in us today; we declare the word of hope into our lives and into every situation, for you are our healer and our greatest physician. Father God, we will remain forever grateful to you for all that you have bestowed upon us. We declare strength so your children will rise on the wings of eagles. Help us, Lord! We need you! We thank you with all our hearts, and we give you all the praise, honour, and glory for giving us life! For you alone are worthy. In Jesus' name we pray... THANK GOD...

Amen.

NOTES

Heavenly Father, as we rise to see another day, we thank you, praise, glorify, magnify your name. You are good and your mercies endure forever. We thank you for being our strength, our guide and protector. Help us to remember we are your own, and no matter if we feel like we are at the back of the line, God, you can move us to the front. Help us to embrace whatever it is you have in store for us today and the rest of this week; you know what will be best for each and every one of us, and how much we can handle in our life. We ask that you go before us, and make the crooked pathways in our lives straight. Meet the needs of your children, give us the courage and strength to face all that is placed before us, and lead us into the path that is best for us according to your will, your plan and your ways. Help us to remember that every day is a blessing, as the Holy Spirit continues to lead our way. In Jesus' name we pray... THANK GOD...

Amen.

NOTES

Father, we thank you for waking us up to another great day. We pray that you be with us all day long, strengthen us, equip us, and prepare us for what we will face today. Help us to keep our peace, our joy. Help us to have a forgiving heart, Lord Jesus. Help us to remember to keep our eyes focused on you and your word, not on things or people, and open our ears to listen to the Holy Spirit when you speak to us. Father God, you are the goal and the aim, and you are what we are reaching out for at all times. Help us to take refuge in you, and let us pour out our hearts to you. Keep us in the centre of your will and the palm of your hand today. We are victorious, we are more than conquerors, and we can do all things through Christ who loves us. Thank you, Father, for hearing our prayers. In Jesus' name we pray... THANK GOD...

Amen.

NOTES

Lord, we give you praise and honour. We glorify and magnify your name, and we are thankful for your goodness this morning. We give you all our concerns and worries, and ask that you fill us with your peace and confidence as we go through this day. We trust and know you are with us, and you are willing and able to make a way where at times we feel there is none. Father, direct our minds and thoughts according to your purposes, and fill us with your faith today. We know if we continue to hold on to your hands, we will reach our destination. We pray that you forgive us when we don't thank you enough for who you are, for all that you do, and all that you have given us. Help us to keep our eyes and our hearts set on you daily, keep our spirit renewed, and keep us filled with your joy and peace. Thank you, Father, for all you have done for us, for shielding, protecting and providing for us, and for making ways. We give you all honour and praise because it's already yours. In Jesus' mighty name... THANK GOD...

Amen.

NOTES

1. No Man is an Island

Father, in the mighty name of Jesus we thank you for waking us up to another day, and bringing us once again to a new week. We lift up our hands this morning to praise, worship and magnify, and glorify your name; you are the same yesterday, today and forever. You will always be our healer, our miracle worker, deliverer, our way, and we thank you, Lord, you never fail. Lord, we trust in you, in your name, in your power and your provision. Only you know what today's needs will be, so we ask that you use our lives as a vessel of love, of faith, and the purpose that you have laid out for each and every one of us. Help us to come out of agreements that aren't pleasing in your sight, Lord. Help us to live a righteous life, and to do the things that are pleasing not just by you, but by others. We are not in this world by ourselves, no man is an island, so Father, help us to be mindful of the people that are around us; to be helpful, to be kind, to show love, to forgive and forget when people have wronged us. Father God, let your presence go forth with us, keep us energised with your strength to do more, and help us to put all our trust in you today. In Jesus' mighty name we pray.... THANK GOD...

Amen.

NOTES

2. You Can Count on the Promises of God

Heavenly Father, you're so good, so gracious, so kind, so marvellous, so wonderful, and so strong, and we thank you for life. You carry all our worries, our pain, our tears, our trials and tribulations on your shoulder, and you never give up on us. As you promise us you will never leave us nor forsake us, we must cast all our cares to you, so we thank you for being our rock, our healer and provider. We thank you for our ups and downs, and your grace and mercy that we don't deserve, Lord Jesus.

We thank you for covering and comforting us. We thank you for your word and your promises. Father, we know that we will have days of darkness that will hover over us, leaving us wondering which way to turn, or which way to go, so today we ask and pray that you reveal your path for us, shine your light upon us and be a lamp to our feet. Fill us with your Holy Spirit, and help us to see the signs you have set for us so that we can follow you safely through life, trusting in you completely. Thank you for hearing our prayers, and working on the answers, even if we don't always know all the details of your plan for each of our lives. In Jesus' name we pray... THANK GOD...

Amen.

NOTES

Hear our cry, O God, attend to our prayer. From the end of the earth we will cry to you. When our heart is overwhelmed, lead us to the rock that is higher than high, for you have been a shelter for us, a strong tower from the enemy...

Father, we lift our hands to you this morning. We praise, honour, glorify and love you, Lord. If it was not for your grace to us, there's no way we would be here, and we are so thankful you have never given up on us, Lord. Father, we know you sit high above all others, and looking down on us today teach us to do your will. Give us the grace to be helpers of each other's spiritual good, and be of good grace to others. Open our heart to the Holy Spirit that we may receive a new spirit of love as we go through the day. Keep us from falling, Lord God, let no hurt come to us. Shield us from temptation, and pour upon us your grace and love, as we bow at your feet and lay our burdens down. Lord, let us keep knocking at your door, because we know you will open that door and lead us through. This we ask in the precious name of our Lord and Saviour Jesus Christ...

THANK GOD...

Amen.

NOTES

My dear Heavenly Father, today we lift up our eyes to the hills from where our help comes. Our help comes from you, Lord, who made Heaven and Earth. Lord, we lift up everyone under the sound of our voice this morning, may they be drawn to your presence and dwell in the secret place of the most high. We pray that everyone will be covered, protected, secured, defended, shielded, and hidden by your shadow and hidden from the hand of the enemy; the devil will not lay his hand on them or their families, and even when the enemy tries to steal our joy, may he fail and be crushed by the angels of the Lord which encamp around all who fear him. Father God, give us peace of mind; let it be your will in our soul and our home. Father, we claim your word and say surely goodness and mercy shall follow us all the days of our lives. We claim victory in the name of Jesus; victory over any mountains or obstacles set by the enemy. Father, we choose to trust in you each day, each hour and every moment in our life. You are holy and awesome, and we give you all the glory, honour and praise because it's already yours. In Jesus' mighty name... THANK GOD...

Amen.

NOTES

_____

_____

_____

Heavenly Father, we bow before you and your son King Jesus, giving you thanks for another day and the end of another week. All praise, glory and honour belongs to you. You are our redeemer and saviour. Lord, we know with you on our side, we will be always standing victorious when the battle is over. Help us to realise the greatness that you have placed on the inside of us. Father, break the chains of anything that tries to hold us down from praising you. We lift our hands as a sign of us relinquishing all control to you this morning. Help us to remain focused and committed to doing whatever it is that you call upon us to do, never becoming discouraged or having the will to quit. Have mercy upon us, Lord Jesus, hide us into your shadow where there is love, because with your love there's no pain, no fear, and no sorrow. Your love banishes all negativity, Lord Jesus, and in you we will put our trust. You are the Kings of Kings, and Lord above all Lords, the Alpha and Omega, there's none like you in all the universe. So we thank you, Lord, for all that you do. In Jesus' mighty name we pray... THANK GOD...

Amen.

NOTES

_____

_____

_____

Week Thirty-Nine

1. He Is Always Watching Over Us

Lord, we thank you for another brand new week. Thank you for the grace to begin again. Thank you for being our present help in time of trouble. Thank you for helping us to stand strong. Thank you for covering us, and keeping us safe from all hurt, harm and dangers. So on this day, Father God, we pray that you watch over us, keep us with a clear mind, open eyes, and open ears to hear your voice. Help us to pay close attention to the true signs of the Holy Spirit that you bring to us, so that our life will change for the better. Lord, we know that there's no place that we can go outside of your loving eyes, because you are always watching over us, and you are always there for us when we need your help and support. Create in us a clean heart and purify us so that we may do all that you want us to do. Father, you are Jehovah Rapha, the Lord God that heals, so Lord, we ask today that you heal the earth, strengthen those who are weak, and give peace to those who are walking in worry and doubt. Thank you, Father God, for hearing and answering our prayers. In Jesus' name we pray...THANK GOD...

Amen.

NOTES

Heavenly Father, we thank you, we praise, magnify, and glorify your name. Thank you for allowing us to wake up and see the beauty and goodness of all your creations on this new day. We love you because you died on the cross for our sins. Thank you for the strength, and the wisdom that you will give us for your provision. Open our eyes and our hearts to who you really are, God. Father, we have no knowledge of what the day holds, or what the days ahead may bring, so help us to face all that we encounter head on, and get through the days with your power and your strength. We give you all the praise, honour and glory that you deserve. Maintain our faith and trust in all that you do. Keep each of us in good health, and daily strength while you lead us beside still water and restore our soul. Restore hope and peace in our journey of life, and let your word come alive in us today. In Jesus' mighty name we pray... THANK GOD...

Amen.

NOTES

Heavenly Father, Our King and Saviour, thank you for your mercy and grace upon our lives today. This is the day you have made and we will be glad and rejoice in it. Father, we place this day into your hand; lead us not into temptation, but deliver us from all evil. Help us to keep a clear and stable mind, and may all that we say and do be pleasing to you. Lord, as we step out today, we ask for travelling mercies, clear and cut all dangers ahead of us, and keep us safe under the shadow of your wings. Keep our faith strong in you, and help us not to be afraid. If we encounter any situation that will bring fear in our mind, help us to put our faith and trust in you, Father God. We receive your grace and mercy, so we can be a vessel used by you. Help us to wait patiently on you, and be obedient to your word, because in the fullness of our time you will answer our prayers. We give you all the praise, honour, and glory. In Jesus' mighty name we pray... THANK GOD...

Amen.

NOTES

_____

_____

_____

_____

Heavenly and Mighty Father, today we call you the great I Am. We surrender everything to you; our spirit, body and soul. All praise, glory and honour belongs to you this morning, King Jesus. Father, we lift our hands as a sign of relinquishing our praise to you. We thank you for your goodness and mercy, for fighting all our battles both seen and unseen, and for guiding all our decisions and actions with your divine wisdom. Father God, let our words be in line with your words, and help us to see the manifestation of your word come to pass in our lives, that it would be like a fire in our bones. Help us today, Father God; may your light become the light that shines your love to others through this dark world we are living in. We know you are alive, Lord, you are sitting high above and watching over us. Lord, let this be a day of success, and bring completion to all that we hoped for, a day in which we receive healing, peace, and joy. This we receive in faith, and we thank you for it. In Jesus' mighty name we pray... THANK GOD...

Amen.

NOTES

_____

_____

_____

_____

_____

Father, in the mighty name of Jesus, we thank you for bringing us to the end of another week. Many things could have gone against us, Father God, and we thank you for your protection, faithfulness, goodness, grace and mercy. Mighty God, take over our mind, cover our families, our children, our friends, everyone we pass by today and in our future in the mighty name of Jesus. Father, as we lift our head to you, we ask that you revive us, revive our prayers, our life, and our relationship with you. Have your way in our life today and the days ahead, for you are our strength, and shield, and we will forever praise you, Father God. Order our steps and help us to walk confidently with you by our side. Keep us forever reminded to never cease praying, because we know and believe that the power of prayer changes all things. We thank you now in advance for knowing that your help and provision for us has no limits and no boundaries. In Jesus' mighty name we pray... THANK GOD...

Amen.

NOTES

_____

_____

_____

_____

Week Forty

1. Lord, Comfort Our Hearts

Heavenly Father, we thank you for waking us to this new day, feeling grateful to you for giving us life, loving ourselves as we are and how you created us, and having love and care in our hearts for our children, families and dear friends. Father, the hearts and mind of so many of us are shattered, torn, and left in despair by unfortunate events that have taken place in our lives at the hands of others, or even our enemy. So today we lift our hands to you, Father God, asking you to restore our faith. Help us to forgive all those who have judged, wronged, or hurt us in ways that are inhumane. Lord, even though anger, bitterness, and malice still lingers in our hearts, help us to not have vengeful thoughts, or speak anything that is not of you, or not pleasing to you. Comfort our hearts, bring peace, and uplift and encourage us to do what is right in you. With a caring heart, we thank you for hearing and answering our prayers. In Jesus' name we pray... THANK GOD...

Amen.

NOTES

Heavenly Father, we love you, thank you, glorify, and magnify you this morning, and as we lift our hands in praise, let your glory fill the house. Lord, we know we are not living in a perfect world, but we know you are a God who provides, heals, and blesses, and a God who is always worthy and deserving of praise. We know you will withhold no good thing from those who love you. You said you would not deny your help to any of your people who ask, and for that we are thankful. Father, our hearts are crying out for you; give us the assurance that you are by our side, because you are one who can turn things around for our good. Father God, we know you always do things even in the darkest hour, it is for us to only be patient and put our trust in you. So we thank you in advance for all blessings that you have bestowed upon us. Thank you for being our God of miracles, our God of wonders, and for this we will always and forever remain grateful to you. Today let your peace rest upon us, and give us a reason to be joyful, as the Holy Spirit continues to lead our way. In Jesus' name we pray... THANK GOD...

Amen.

NOTES

_____

_____

_____

Lord Jesus the Almighty one, who made Heaven and Earth. We thank you for brand new mercies this morning, this is the day you have made, we will be glad and rejoice in it. Lord, on this day we thank you for your grace and mercy upon our lives. Teach us to be more trusting in you, and help us to build our faith. Let the Holy Spirit teach us and remind us that the trials and troubles we face, and the pain we feel can be a blessing in disguise. Lord, we know sometimes you use our troubles to remind us that you are our saviour, our deliverer, our hope, and rescuer, the chief cornerstone to all of our problems. Father, give us the grace to remain positive, and hopeful in you, Lord Jesus, because the trials we face are temporary, and they are pale in comparison to the joy you have awaiting us. Help us to stand strong and not be defeated; because you are strong over Satan, we know we can be victorious over the devil, and walk in victory in Jesus' name. Enlighten our spirit, so that we see through the light of faith. Open the floodgate of Heaven in our lives today and the rest of this week. In Jesus' mighty name we pray... THANK GOD...

Amen.

NOTES

Lord, we have so much to be thankful for this morning. First and foremost we give you thanks for our life, that we can wake up and see our loved ones. Help us to embrace and rejoice in all that the day holds, because we know that tomorrow is not promised, but through your grace, love, and mercy you will continue to surround us with your powerful presence. Let your lamp be a light unto our path. Help us to keep our eyes focused on you, and open our ears to listen and follow your instructions at all times. Father God, we surrender our life and place all our concerns into your mighty hands, for we trust you will direct us to do all that pleases you. Keep our loved ones, our homes under your protective care, and may we speak words that bring life over ourselves and to others. We pray for divine strength, health, and favour to make it through this day with the blood of Jesus continuing to cover us. Let the enemy see and know without doubt that you go before us, and that you have our back. We give you all the praise, honour, and glory in Jesus' mighty name... THANK GOD...

Amen.

NOTES

_____

_____

_____

Father, we are blessed this morning to wake up and see the rising of the sun, the beauty of this day, and to breathe the fresh air; for this we are so grateful. We thank you for your unconditional love, and the many blessings you've given us. Thank you for being our refuge and fortress in times of trouble. Please help us to cast all our cares to you, and turn our worries into prayers. Father, we trust you are working things out for our good. Thank you for your goodness and faithfulness in our lives.

Today we pray in faith for all those who are sick – physically, mentally, emotionally – and for those who are suffering from domestic abuse. Lord, please touch them with your healing hand and restore full health. Speak to the heart of the abusers, God, and let them know they can find comfort in you. Take away every burden of pain and anguish from them, and cleanse them, Father God. Create in them a clean and pure heart, Lord Jesus. We pray for our doctors, nurses, and carers; give them your strength, courage, wisdom and provision. Keep each and every one safe and in good health. Help us to stay strong in your faith throughout these difficult days we're living in, as the Holy Spirit continues to lead our way. In Jesus' name we pray... THANK GOD...

Amen.

NOTES

Week Forty-One

1. Nothing Can Change God's Love for Us

Father, you hear our hearts this morning, give us your heart, your love, your peace and your joy. Thank you for blessing us with another day, and for taking us through the last seven days. Your love is everlasting, your love never fails, and it fuels our faith. We want to love the way you love us, Father God. Keep our hearts fixed on you today, and help us to live the life you want us to live, forgiving others, and forgetting the past, so we can look ahead and live in love, and dwell in your promises. You gave your life because of the love you have for us, and we are so grateful. Thank you for the power of the Holy Spirit that speaks to us, rejoices in us. Have your way in our lives today, as we surrender our hearts, minds, our will, and emotions to you. We wait on you, our hearts are opened; we need direction and clarity, and we ask that you take full control. Help us to rejoice and be glad in you, Lord God, the great Almighty. Hold us in the palm of your hand, guide our steps today, and deepen our relationship with you. In Jesus' mighty name we pray... THANK GOD...

Amen.

NOTES

_____

_____

_____

Heavenly Father, you are the Jehovah Rapha – our healer. As we wake up to this brand new day, we thank you for letting us be on the wake-up list this morning. Thank you for the blessings you have prepared for us this week. Direct our steps today by your word, Father God, and let no iniquity have dominion over us (Psalms 119:133). We come to you with a humble heart, asking you to heal our health problems that have drained us of our strength, physically, mentally, and spiritually. Father God, give us your strength, and let your anointing flow in and throughout our whole body. Father, we trust and believe in your word, which says "and by His stripes we are healed." Rebuild and increase our faith, fill us with your Holy Spirit, and help us to put our trust in you. Enable and equip us with all that is needed, as we seek to carry out the plan and purpose that you have for us today, and the rest of this week. Continue to strengthen us for whatever lies ahead, and keep us covered with the precious blood of Jesus. And all God's children said praise the Lord!

Amen.

NOTES

3. God's "Agape" Love

Father, in the mighty name of Jesus, we thank you for blessing us with another beautiful day. Thank you for knowing and assuring us that your mercies are new every morning, and shall follow us all the days of our lives. Today we ask that you go before us and make our crooked path straight, strengthen us where we are weak, and make a way where sometimes there seems to be no way. Today, Father God, we ask that you lead us into greener pastures, and doors that are closed in our lives open them so that we can walk boldly through this journey of life. Calm our fears and give us the peace and answers to our problems. Help us to love those who are broken hearted, as you love them with the "agape" love you have for us all, which is unconditional. Please keep us lifted into your righteous hand, and allow us to stand on your foundation for strength, knowing that it will never be shaken. We thank you, praise, love and adore you, Father, and we give you all the glory. In Jesus' mighty name we pray... THANK GOD...

Amen.

NOTES

_____

_____

_____

_____

_____

Father, in the mighty name of Jesus, we thank you, for you have filled our life with supernatural grace and favour. Nothing will be impossible to us with you by our side. Lord, we trust that you are bigger than our problems and you are working on our behalf. Touch each and every one of us under the sound of our voice this morning, keep us in the centre of your will and the palm of your hands. Help us to keep our eyes on you and remain forever grateful for our families, for the roof over our heads, the food we eat, and the job that you have kept us in, because Lord, so many are in need, and we believe that you will supply all our needs according to your richness in glory. So Father, we thank you for providing, for fighting our battles, and for leading us. Give us the strength to endure and grow in faith in these difficult times. Calm our fears, and give us the peace and the answers we need today. Use our life for your glory. In Jesus' name we pray... THANK GOD...

Amen.

NOTES

Father God, we thank you for waking us up to this brand new day. We are blessed and glad to be alive, and amongst the living. Thank you for strengthening our mind and our body. Father, your word tells us that "they that wait on the Lord shall renew their strength", so Father renew our strength, so that we may mount upon wings like an eagle; we will run and not be weary, we will walk and not get faint. Lord, we are praying today for the weary, and for those who are broken hearted; strengthen us in the name of Jesus. Heal our minds and our souls. Help us to realise that our hope and strength is in you, Father, our faith is in you, not our situation. Teach us to centre our life on you, so that we may live our lives in a way that brings honour to your name. We pray that you give us renewed strength, strong faith and a peaceful mind, and keep us filled with your supernatural power, to face and overcome every obstacle that we encounter today. Father God, give us the assurance that you will never leave us nor forsake us. Where you lead we will follow without question, and we will trust that our life is in your hands. In Jesus' mighty name... THANK GOD...

Amen.

NOTES

1. Help Us Walk in Obedience

Father, in the mighty name of Jesus, we thank you for bringing us to the beginning of another week. Father, you're good and your mercies endure forever. We thank you for being a way-maker, miracle worker, promise keeper and the light when we see darkness. Father God, you are everything we need, just when we need it, and we thank you for it. Father, we lean, trust and depend on you; we give you glory and honour; we don't let our faith waver, we stand firm on your word that you will take care of us. Help us to walk in obedience, and may every step we take be a step of faith in you, Lord Jesus. Father, we thank you for giving us the direction we need for our lives this week. We believe and trust you are at work in us. We surrender all we have this week, and we thank you for leading, providing and fighting our battles. We receive everything you have for us by faith today, and may we receive all the blessings you have in store for us throughout the week. In Jesus' mighty name we pray... THANK GOD...

Amen.

NOTES

_____

_____

_____

Heavenly Father, we thank you for another sunrise; we made it, and as we opened our eyes it brought us hope. No matter how good or bad yesterday was, you woke us up this morning and we are thankful. We declare that Jesus is our Lord and Saviour, and you died on the cross so we can live a life of joy and peace. We are thankful for your goodness and mercy that will follow us all the days of our lives. Thank you for the strength, power, love and the authority, not with the devil, but over our enemy. Lord, we cancel everything he will send our way, we push back the darkness, and we welcome the power and the presence of you in our lives. We thank you, Father God, for carrying us through the hard times; we know you will never leave us, you are our present help in all situations. Help us to love others as you do, and not to do anything with selfish motives. Help us to stay focused on you today, and throughout this week, and live with the joy that comes from knowing you. Help us to share your love, and goodness as we experience your peace, power and presence throughout this day. We thank you for equipping us to do great things, because every good and perfect gift is from you, Father God. You get all the glory, you get all the praise, and we give you everything. Thank you for blessing everyone this morning, In Jesus' mighty name we pray... THANK GOD...

Amen.

NOTES

Father, in the name of Jesus, we come before you humble as we can be, giving you thanks and praise for another day. We thank you for waking us up to be alive in Christ, because you are our Lord and Saviour, and we give you all the praise, honour and glory. We receive all your blessings and your presence in our lives for today and the rest of this week. Father, help us to walk with your peace that surpasses all understanding, with the power and knowledge that we are blessed. Father God, please let your presence go before us on our journey. We know that your mighty hand is there to protect us if there's anything seen or unseen weighing us down, or hindering us from moving forward to draw us closer to you. We pray that you remove it, unleashing every stronghold, and breaking every chain. Please let your mercy sustain and strengthen us, and in your mercy help us to stand with you. Have mercy on our families and dear friends, as they walk out on their journey of life with you by their side. Help us not to be fearful about what tomorrow will bring, because we put our future, our hope, and our dreams into your mighty hands, and we trust you will fulfil your plans and purposes in our life. So help us to rejoice and be exceedingly glad, for we are sons and daughters set free by the blood of Jesus Christ... THANK GOD...

Amen.

NOTES

4. Pour Out Your Blessings Around the World

Lord Jesus, we thank you and praise you for waking us up to another day. Thank you for grace, mercy, and salvation. Thank you for everything that you have made available to us – we are so grateful. Father, help us to live our life according to your will, go before us and make every crooked path straight. You said eye has not seen, nor ear heard, and no human has conceived the things you have prepared for us. Today we ask you to meet the needs of each and every one of us. Pour out your spirit and blessings around the world, Lord Jesus; may you comfort those who are mourning their loved ones, heal us, fill us with hope, and give us your peace. We pray for all the leaders of this world, whomever and wherever they may be; anoint them as you fill them with your divine wisdom to lead your people, Father God. We pray on the health, finance, and well-being of all your children; may your will be done in our lives today. Father, help us to live and love right, help us to treat others kindly, help us to forgive and forget all the hurt and pain of our past, and help us to remember we are all yours. We speak life, healing, deliverance, salvation and peace. May the peace of God be with us throughout today, and the rest of this week. In Jesus' mighty name we pray... THANK GOD...

Amen.

NOTES

Father, as we come to another week, we come to you not in need but with a thankful heart, for you are good and your mercies endure forever. Lord, we thank you for the sacrifice that you made for us, and for the love and mercy you continue to have for us all. We thank you and praise you, Father God, we want more of you. Help us to refocus and align our hearts and minds to draw closer to you, because you are our source and all that we need. Lord, too often we choose to pursue momentary things and push you aside; please forgive us, and change us, and help to live our life focused on you. Show us the steps to take to refocus our hearts and minds on you alone. Search our hearts, Father God, see if there be any wicked ways in us; cleanse us from every sin and set us free. Father, show us the path that leads to life, and fill us with joy in your presence. We love you and we want to fix our eyes on you. We receive your mercy and grace today, so we will live a life that is pleasing to you. Thank you for always providing for us. In Jesus' mighty name we pray... THANK GOD...

Amen.

NOTES

Week Forty-Three

1. A New Level of Knowing You

Lord, we thank you for waking us up; we are still in the land of the living and we are grateful. Father God, we acknowledge you this morning through our prayers and worship. May our steps be ordered and directed by you. Lord, give us the wisdom and insight concerning our affairs, and let us be a blessing to all those around us; no matter what happens today, we know you will see us through. We stand on your words to lead and guide us to "acknowledge you and you shall direct our paths" (Proverbs 3:6), so go before us today, Lord Jesus, and clear all dangers that are ahead of us. We choose to honour you, Father God, by the words that we speak, and allow your love and your light to shine through us. Fill us with your Holy Spirit, your joy, the knowledge of your son, root us and ground us in love, so we know the love of Christ. We are the head and not the tail, and we are above, and not beneath, we are blessed coming in and going out. Open the eyes of our understanding so we can see who you are, and grow in knowledge of you. We choose to walk in your revelation, and come after you because you love us. Help us to walk in a new level of knowing you, Father God, and let our hearts be submitted to you. In Jesus' mighty name we pray... THANK GOD...

Amen.

NOTES

Father God, we thank you, praise you, magnify, and glorify you. O, Lamb of God who was crucified for our sins, you bled and died, precious is your blood. You are good and your mercies endure forever, you are strong, mighty, loving and a righteous God. Today we come against the lies of the enemy that would make us think that God doesn't love and care for us, but we know you do. Thank you for equipping us, and for lighting the way. We know that your yoke is easy and your burden is light, for every step we take, every door that we have to go through you go through it with us today, Lord Jesus. We thank you for moving us in the right direction, so we get on the right path with you; not the path of what we think or what we feel, but your path, your perfect plan for our lives. We thank you for the hope and the future you have for us. Search our hearts and purge us, create in us a clean and pure heart, so we can search you out and seek you first. Remove pride, and increase our love for one another. We thank you for your promise of protection and provision. We are your sheep. Teach us to trust and follow your leading all the days of our lives. In your name, Jesus... THANK GOD...

Amen.

NOTES

Heavenly Father, it is a blessing to wake up each morning and to always call upon your Holy Name. We don't deserve your love and mercy, but you keep giving us more than we ask for. Your goodness and mercy are on us all, Father God, and we know that you have all our names written in the palm of your mighty hand. Lord, as we rise this morning, we commit this day into your powerful hands. We are your sheep, and we ask that you lead us today into the path of righteousness. Father, for each and every person under the sound of our voice, guide and protect them, keep them covered by the blood of Jesus, and care for their families and friends. Father, if they've gone far away from you, draw their hearts back to you. Lord, if they put their trust in other things, help them to realise that our hope and our trust should lie on you. Let your Holy Spirit bring calmness to our hearts in every situation we will face this week. Let your will be done and grant us the grace to understand and accept your will for our lives. In Jesus' mighty name we pray... THANK GOD...

Amen.

NOTES

Thank you, Father God, for your goodness this morning. Your grace and mercy has brought us through to another day. Father God, your word says "the righteous cry out, and the Lord hears" (Psalms 34:17-18). Hear our cry today, Father God, and deliver us from all our troubles. We lift everyone this morning, Lord, hear our cry, do not pass us by. In every moment of desperation we know we can call upon you, Lord Jesus, we know when we call upon your name, Lord, there's freedom, rescue, refuge, healing, and hope. You are merciful and kind, Lord, a God who is always willing to help those who seek you sincerely. Father, so many times we take up things upon ourselves and push you aside, so this day we ask for your forgiveness; help us to invite you in all that we do and say. Let us turn to you instead of trying to do things on our own because we are weak on our own, but with you we are strong; we are made whole and led by your Holy Spirit. Lord, let all we do today be perfected by your blessing and bring glory and honour to your holy name. Thank you for hearing our prayer. In the mighty and matchless name of Jesus Christ we pray... THANK GOD...

Amen.

NOTES

_____

_____

_____

Heavenly Father, we come to you this morning with our hearts willing and open, giving you thanks for another day, and for bringing us again through another week. This weekend set us to walk in love and to receive your grace and mercy which are new each and every morning. Father, help us to put all our trust in you, not our emotions or anxiety. You didn't give us a spirit of fear, you gave us power, love and a sound mind, so we thank you, God, help us do what is right today. We thank you, God, that you have plans to prosper us, plans to do good not evil. Help us all to remember that without you we are nothing, and our sole purpose is to serve and worship you. Lord, may your presence dwell in our hearts, and when our spirits fall deep, may we witness the shining hope that only your grace can provide. Please be with us, and with all who need your loving touch and your presence. And all God's children said praise the Lord! THANK GOD...

Amen.

NOTES

_____

_____

_____

_____

Week Forty-Four

1. A Day of New Opportunities

Father, with you is not another day, it's a day of new opportunities, another chance, a new beginning, a new week. How great you are, Father God! Lord, we pray as we enter into this new week it will bring peace, miracles, healing, deliverance, and favour. May you continue to bless and protect us, and keep us covered under the blood of Jesus. Draw us closer to you, lead and guide us, open doors that are closed, and let your Holy Spirit lead the way. Help us to order our days to live our life to the fullest, and to take nothing for granted. Lord, we pray for all those who are in need; never let them go without, continue to supply all their needs according to your riches in glory. Comfort those who are hurting, bring hope to the hopeless, and rest for the weary. We are forever grateful for all the blessings you have for us; your promises, and most of all your great love for us. We bless you, magnify and glorify you, knowing that you have good plans for us. Help us to focus on you this month and let nothing steal the joy you have for us. I thank you that we will be satisfied with you and you alone, not people, not things, but God. Our satisfaction comes from you, because you give us what we need. We pray the forces of Heaven answer our prayers this new week. In Jesus' mighty and precious name... THANK GOD...

AMEN.

NOTES

2. The Name of the Lord is a Strong Tower

Thank you, dear Lord, for waking us up to another day. Reveal to us the hidden things in our life that we should get rid of, and show us what choices we should make. Give us wisdom and understanding regarding how we should live our lives, where we should place our energy and focus. As your word says, "the name of the Lord is a strong tower, the righteous run to it and are safe." Lord, we know when we call upon your name it is stronger than any sickness, more powerful than darkness, and bigger than any mountain. Help us to look forward to the future with hope, lift up our spirit today, show up and walk through our homes, rebuke and cancel all things that are not of you. To those who are sick in body, bring them the healing that they have being praying for, as you give them peace. Draw all of us closer to you, as the Holy Spirit continues to lead our way. Thank you for the grace you have given us, and let us know we can walk with you. Thank you for giving us the freedom to worship you each day; so many are crying out to you and are not able to do so, reach out to them, Father, because we live in a free world. Take away all our worries, pain, sickness, and continue to bless us. Lift up your light and countenance upon us today. In Jesus' name we pray... THANK GOD...

Amen.

NOTES

Father God, we thank you for another day; you're good and your mercies endure forever. We thank you for your strength, purpose, love, deliverance, and salvation. We thank you that today will be a day of victory, a day of overcoming, and a day of walking in peace that surpasses all understanding. On this day, Lord, keep us enlightened and reminded of the greatness of your power. We pray that you remove everything from our lives that is not pleasing to your sight, and make all things new, healing us from our sickness, blessing us with your riches in glory, clarifying our negative situations and bringing us peace and love in the midst of it all. Glorious God, we praise your name, we wear your crown and we worship you. We thank you, Father, so we can abide in the secret place of the most high and to get to know you. You are faithful, and you made a way for us. Let us speak pleasant words of life to others, so we can experience life in return. Lord, you are amazing, you are always listening, you never lock us out, we can dial your name and you are always there to answer. Be the Lord of our life, create in us a clean heart, and a right spirit. In Jesus' name... THANK GOD...

Amen.

NOTES

_____

_____

_____

Heavenly Father, our Saviour and Redeemer, we thank you for your grace and your mercy. We thank you for your loving kindness, we thank you for being with us, and for blessing us. It's not an easy road, Lord Jesus, but through you we can do all things. Keep us in the centre of your will and the palm of your hand. Order our steps in everything we do, and everywhere we go, guide us and lead us for you are our good shepherd. Your word says in Psalms 23:3: "He restores my soul, He leads me in the paths of righteousness for His name's sake." Help us to embrace whatever comes our way with faith in the knowledge that you are greater than any storm or situation we may face. Your agape love displaces all fear, it dispels all darkness, so we praise, honour and glorify your name. May your Holy Spirit continue to empower us to stand firm and stand strong. Thank you, Lord, for being with us each and every day, cover us with your blood, Jesus. Thank you for hearing our prayers. In Jesus' name we pray... THANK GOD...

Amen.

NOTES

Father, as we face this day and the weekend ahead, we pray you grant each of us the strength, energy, and courage we need to take us through the day, as we seek your face, your comfort and your peace. Help us to stand strong in faith against the strategies of the devil, greater is He that is in me than he that is in the world. You are greater than sickness, disease, poverty, lack, and the forces of darkness. We are overcomers, with prayers, your words, and the armour of God. Help us to stay focused on you, and let our worries fall by the wayside, so that our hearts may be filled with joyful praises unto you each and every day. For your word says: "Be anxious for nothing, but in everything by prayer and supplication, with thanksgiving, let your request made known to God." (Philippians 4:6) Help us to stand strong in faith, knowing that your promises to us will be fulfilled. We know you are the God of truth and the blessings will come our way... THANK GOD...

Amen.

NOTES

Week Forty-Five

1. The Prayer of the Righteous Man Prevails

Dear God, you are our hiding place, our strong tower, and under your wings we can always find refuge. We thank you for raising us up to a brand new day, and bringing us to another week. Help us to walk in your light, touch our hearts and make us an instrument of your peace. Help us to know your ways, teach us to do your will, and walk on your path. We are grateful for your Holy Spirit, your words and your promises to us, Father God, which you use to set us free from worry and give us peace. Lord, we find comfort knowing you are by our side. We come through the fire and through the rain, and you have never left us out, so we can face whatever is ahead of us. Father God, we give you all the praise, honour, and glory, because we know you are equipping us for good. You have promised us that you will walk with us all the days of our lives, even when we feel we are wrapped up in chains. The fervent prayer of the righteous man avails much (James 5:16), so we will continue to lift up your name, Jesus, because it's bigger and greater than any other names. Open doors of opportunity in our lives today, as your Holy Spirit continues to lead. In Jesus' mighty name we pray... THANK GOD...

Amen.

NOTES

Father, we stretch our hands to thee, no other help we've known, and if you draw thyself from thee, then rather shall we go. Lord, help us to believe and trust in you knowing you are the great I Am. As your word says in Job 42:2, "I know that you can do everything, and that no purpose of yours can be withheld from you," so today we ask you to guide us on our steps in and out, keep us in the centre of your will and the palm of your hand. Let your light shine in us, Father God, you have never failed nor forsaken us, even in difficult times, we know you can open and make a way when there seems to be none. Stand on our behalf today, let your presence be strong in our lives. Father God, we lift up our children and teachers as they head to school today, bring forth an abundance of blessings and favour on them, Lord Jesus. Keep them covered by your blood. Bless the teachers, keep them assured that no matter what they are facing, your heart is towards them, your eyes are watching over each and every one, and your ears are listening to our prayers. Father, help us to make good decisions for ourselves and our loved ones this week. We receive your grace and mercy so that we can be a vessel used by you. In Jesus' name... THANK GOD...

Amen.

NOTES

Father, we glorify, and worship you. We adore your holy name, and we give you all the praise. Gracious and Heavenly Father, on this day we ask that you empower us with the Holy Spirit, and in our weakness please give us your strength to help us through the unbearable situations and circumstances that we face; Lord, we cannot do it alone. Let your light shine through our lives, and help us to remember you can and you will. Thank you, Father, for seeing us as valuable, help us to see ourselves as you see us; you see us as righteous and royal in your eyes, as your word says, "we are fearfully and wonderfully made" in your image. You know the inner workings of our heart, and we ask you to remove anything that is not of you. If we walk in the wrong way, forgive us, God. Thank you for your powerful presence in our lives, and we can be assured that no matter what we are facing, your heart is towards us, and your eyes are watching over us, and we are safe in your care. Keep us covered with your blood, and safe in your hands. We thank you and bless your holy name, you are so worthy of our praise, and there's none like you. Have your way in our lives. In Jesus' mighty name we pray... THANK GOD...

Amen.

NOTES

Heavenly Father, we direct our prayers to you this morning. Hear our cry, listen to our heart, and bless us by your divine grace. As we live by your word, we should always pray and not faint (Luke 18:1). We pray you take away the feelings of anxiety, doubt, and fear, and please provide us with the grace to trust you in all situations. Father, we all need you and your presence in our lives. Help us to remain strong, and to keep our faith and Godly attitude so that we will always glorify your name throughout each and every day you've blessed us with. Father God, please cover, keep and guide us. We thank you that our ears are opened, ready to hear your directions, guidance, and corrections, because we know it's for our good. Fill us and fuel us with everything we need. God, we trust and believe you've given us the victory over everything that the enemy has sent our way to defeat us. He has no power, authority or place in our lives. In Jesus' mighty name we pray... THANK GOD...

Amen.

NOTES

_____

_____

_____

_____

5. *Everlasting Father*

Heavenly Father, as you lift up our heads this morning, we praise your name; your name is blessed, your name is high. Father, we honour you, giving ourselves as a living sacrifice. Let your spirit guide and lead us. We all belong to your kingdom, we have the right to give you all the praise today, as we place our lives in your hands. Father, we need manifestation of your divine intervention and order in our lives, so today we ask that you calm our hearts, and minds, and help us to boldly trust that you are in control when we are in despair. We pray for your strength to help us face our battles, to get through our losses, seen and unseen, and to unify and bind broken relationships. Help us realise you are a faithful, understanding, and everlasting Father; you never fail nor forsake us. Give us peace and bright hope for our days and future, knowing that your grace, mercy, hope and strength are new every morning. We thank you for your wonderful, unconditional love, care, and forgiveness, and from this day forward may we never cease to praise you with our whole heart, and live our whole life for you. As we wait patiently and expectantly, open our doors, Father God, so you can move through. Keep everyone under the sound of our voice safe, and under your wings. In Jesus' mighty name we pray... THANK GOD...

Amen.

NOTES

Week Forty-Six

1. Thank You for the Gift of Life

Dear God, we thank you for giving us the gift of life, for bringing us to another week. Thank you for being our light of the world, our good shepherd, the way, the truth, the light, and our redeemer. As we start this day with love in our hearts, we pray for all those who wake up this morning feeling depressed, and feel like giving up because of the stress in their life. Father, please stand before them and remind them that you are the Almighty Father, a Father who listens and cares for us all. You are the creator of this world, the Alpha and Omega, you're everything we need, and you have everything in control, no matter what lies ahead of us. It's for us to have the faith and cast all our cares into your mighty hand. Be our strong tower, and our resting place. Let every arrow of wickedness return to the sender, let every tongue that rises up against us be condemned in Jesus' mighty name. Thank you for our victory. All the glory and praise belongs to you, Lord Jesus. We will continue to trust in you, and place our faith and our hope in you. You are the one who is, who was, and will forever be, and we thank you for loving us so deeply. In Jesus' mighty name we pray... THANK GOD...

Amen.

NOTES

2. Christ Who Strengthens Us

Almighty Father, we thank you for waking us up to another sunrise. Father God, we depend on your lead today, your energy, strength, and your peace. As we start this day, we ask that you go before us. Keep us safe from all hurt, harm and danger. Equip us and prepare us for what is ahead of us. Help us not to stress today, but let us rely on you completely. Help us to care for and love each other; for those who are in need, and those who are broken and lost. We thank you for your healing power, thank you for healing us from the crown of our head to the soles of our feet. Thank you for your deliverance, provision, and freedom. Please make the crooked or rough pathway that we walk straight and smooth. Keep it clear of all stumbling blocks and barriers. Lead and guide us and grant us wisdom and courage to remove everything that wastes our time, and drains us emotionally, mentally, spiritually and physically. Be our strength, Father God. We thank you for reminding that we can do all things through Christ who strengthens us. (Philippians 4:13) In Jesus' name we ask and pray these things... THANK GOD...

Amen.

NOTES

How can we say thanks for all the things you have done for us? To God be the glory, for all the things you have done. Father, thank you for the privilege to come before you, seeking your guidance and direction over our lives. You continue to bless us with your unconditional love. Father God, we turn over everything to you today, because you are the head of our house. We commit the day and the week to you, and we leave all our plans in your hands. Lord, we depend on your lead; please make a way, and make any crooked pathway straight.

Lord, we pray that today will turn out to be a good day for us all; this is the day you have made, and we will rejoice and be glad in it. Create a new and glorious future for us, no matter how dark our past may have been; we know nothing is too difficult for you, Father God. (Isaiah 43:18-19) Have your way in our lives, perfect all that concerns us and be our daily guide. Draw us closer to you in prayer, and use us for your glory. We pray that the Holy Spirit will do mighty work in us, as you promise us that all things will work together for our good. In Jesus' mighty name we pray... THANK GOD...

Amen.

NOTES

_____

_____

_____

Lord Jesus, we adore you, we lift your name up high; there's none like you. Today will be an amazing day, Father God, because you have made this day. We pray that you increase our faith, and to help us to overcome any disbelief. Help us to walk by faith, not by sight, because as we do so we know that the only thing that matters is you, King Jesus. Father, thank you for equipping us with what we need to live as an overcomer in this life. Help us to always surrender our daily plans to you, we know our lives are in your hands. Lord, we pray that you surround us and our loved ones with your angels of protection as we go through the day; keep the enemy at bay so we can be victorious over every obstacle facing us this week. Thank you that no matter what we are facing, your heart is towards us, your eyes are watching over us, and your ears are opened to our prayers. Let your will be done in our lives. In Jesus' name we pray... THANK GOD...

Amen.

NOTES

5. Father God, We Give You All the Praise

Lord Jesus, we thank you for this day you have woken us up to see. Thank you for allowing your guardian angels to protect us throughout the night. Lord, we pray for everyone under the sound of our voice, giving us another chance, new opportunities, and renewed breath and strength. Fill us with joy and peace as we go through the day. May we not worry or fret about what may happen, but rather submit the day to you in prayer. It is a great comfort to know that with you beside us, and your arms around us we can face whatever lies ahead. Keep us in the path you would have us walk for this coming weekend. Help us not to take for granted the precious gift of life we are blessed to have. Father God, we give you all the praise and glory for your incredible sacrifice so that we have freedom and life. We pray today that unexpected blessings and healing will take place in our lives. In Jesus' name we pray... THANK GOD...

Amen.

NOTES

_____

_____

_____

_____

Week Forty-Seven

1. The Grace to Begin Again

Lord Jesus, we thank you for lifting our heads up to another morning, for bringing us to the beginning of this new week. Thank you for the grace to begin again, and to enjoy this beautiful day, and the countless blessings you have in store for us. Lord, you are our refuge and strength, and no weapon formed against us shall prosper. So today we pray that you touch the hearts of each and every one of us, teach us to live a humble life, so that your light will shine in us. Mould us and make us so that we can become better, stronger, and righteous in your sight. Your word says, "Take my yoke upon you, and learn from me, for I am gentle and humble in heart, and you will find rest for your souls." (Matthew 11:29) As you continue to bless us, Father God, take away our pride so we can walk in humility and reliance upon you. Have mercy upon us because every good and perfect thing comes from you. We continue to put our faith and trust in you alone. Father God, we love you; guide us in the way we should go as we remain focused on you. Help us to walk in love as you love us. In Jesus' name we pray... THANK GOD...

Amen.

NOTES

Father, in the mighty name of Jesus, we would have never made it this morning without you. Thank you for giving us new life. We give you all the glory, honour and praise, because you are great, and there's no one like you. Thank you for your resurrection power that is alive in us. Today we keep our eyes on you, the author and finisher of our faith. Thank you that no matter how dark it looks, our day of breakthrough is on its way. Today, Father God, set us free of every stronghold so that we can live in peace, joy and victory. Thank you for your grace, goodness and mercy, because every good and perfect thing comes from you. Help us to stand firm and put our faith and trust in you and no one else. Father God, we love you so much. Search us and guide us in the way that we should go as we stay focused on you. Keep us forever reminded to humble ourselves before you, for you are great. Thank you for your amazing grace, and for keeping us by your side. You are the Alpha and Omega, the truth and life, the beginning and the end. In Jesus' name we pray... THANK GOD...

Amen.

NOTES

3. *Help us be Good to One Another*

Lord, make us an instrument of your peace; where there is hatred let us sow love; where there is injury, pardon; where there is doubt, faith. Heavenly Father, thank you for your promise of blessings. We agree that all things are possible with you. As we arise this morning, show us our purpose, Lord Jesus. Guide our path and show us what you are leading us to do. We claim healing, deliverance, and blessings over our lives by the authority in the name of Jesus. We pray for you to manifest your supernatural power to turn around every adverse situation in our lives. Heal what you see in our mind, heart, body, and soul, so that we may live a life that is whole and complete. Help us to stand firm on what your word tells us to do. We will abide and rest in you and we thank you for blessing us so we can be a blessing to others. Help us to look out for each other, and understand when we should jump in and help to make a difference. We don't live in this world alone; we are supposed to be good to one another. Help us to do that, Father God. Keep us in the centre of your will and the palm of your hands, and we'll give your name glory, honour, and praise. In Jesus' name we pray... THANK GOD...

Amen.

NOTES

4. We Have Nothing to Fear If We Put Our Trust in God

Our Heavenly Father, we come to you this morning in the mighty name of Jesus, who we belong to, and who we serve. Help us to grow in faith, and find you to be a most trusted and wonderful friend, who is closer than a brother. Father God, open our eyes this day so that we can be believers who bear good fruit, and who will testify about your goodness at every given opportunity. Bring out the best in us, so we can fulfil our purpose in you. Purge our hearts so that we can be gentle, patient, and forgiving to others, as you forgave us. Help us to show love and kindness, and we pray that your Holy Spirit will instil wisdom in us, give us a positive attitude, help us to grow all godliness in us, and remove all things that are not of you, Jesus. Take away pride, anger, and anything negative from our lives, so we can be a vessel for your kingdom, Lord Jesus. Help us to walk in your supernatural peace that surpasses all understanding, and to put our trust in you at all times. Lord, you are a faithful and awesome God, and we love you. We give you all the glory, honour, and praise, in Jesus' mighty name. THANK GOD...

Amen.

NOTES

5. A God Who Cares and Provides

Lord, we thank you for letting us be on the wake-up list this morning, you didn't have to do it, but we're glad you did. Thank you that we are able to see, hear, touch, feel and walk this morning, and that we have a roof over our head. Lord, please provide for those who lack any of these, and let them know you are a God who cares and provides. You will supply all our needs according to your riches in glory. Thank you for your continuous blessing for us, our families and friends. May your son Jesus be the centre of our homes today, and may we be grateful for the beautiful gift of families.

Lord, as we go into the weekend, cover us and our loved ones in the name of Jesus Christ. We declare that we will overcome the enemy by your word, and the blood of the lamb. You are the head of our lives, and you will not make us the tail; we are, and will be blessed in our going out and coming in. So we thank you, Father, for your promises and your protection, because we are more than conquerors. THANK GOD...

Amen.

NOTES

_____

_____

_____

_____

Week Forty-Eight

1. When We Call Upon Your Name

Heavenly Father, we thank you this morning, because you're good and your mercies endure forever. Father, we know that goodness and mercy shall follow us all the days of our lives, and through the power of your name, we will overcome today. Father, we know you are with us; you wake us up for a reason, for new opportunities, and we praise you in advance for all blessings. Father, we don't know what plans you have laid out for us, but we are thankful you are ordering our steps today. We pray that you will do mighty things, will meet our need, and give us that divine intervention in our life. We trust that you will show up at the right time, and step in. We speak the blood of Jesus Christ to break every chain, whether it be in our relationships, our jobs, our health – whatever it may be. We pray that every stronghold will be removed in Jesus' name, because when we call upon your name, Jesus, mountains move, demons tremble, and storms become calm. Father, there's no one greater than you, no one can stand against you. Make a way where there seems to be no way, and through the power of your name we will have victory, and we will rejoice. Lord, we bless your holy name and thank you for listening to our prayers... THANK GOD...

Amen.

NOTES

Heavenly Father, thank you for waking us up this morning, we praise and thank you for another day. Thank you for being in control of our lives, and for the good things you have in store for us. Father, today we rest knowing that our lives are in your hands, knowing that all things are possible with you. Thank you for everyone under the sound of our voice; bless them and keep them in the centre of your will and the palm of your hand. Father, today you know all the families that need extra blessing; those who are going through financial issues, those who are sick, those who are struggling with addiction; you are the greatest physician, our saviour, our strong tower, our provider, and our soon-coming king. We know you will fight our battles for us, Father God, so we cast all our cares to you this morning. Help us to keep a clear and stable mind to make wise choices and decisions, and may your divine wisdom guide us. Unto you O God, we sing our praises. THANK GOD...

Amen.

NOTES

Lord Jesus, we thank you for another day. We thank you that you will be with us today and we will experience your love, joy, and peace. We thank you that you are the way, the truth, and the life. We thank you for guarding and guiding us. You are our strength, our light, our songs, and all that we need. Thank you for being with us through our ups and downs. When we are weak, be our strength, Father God, and speak to our heart, and let us know that you will hold our hands and love us forever. For this we are so grateful.

We look to your word in Deuteronomy 3:23: "We must not fear, for you Lord God will fight for us." Father, you have never lost a battle, and it is you and your word in which we place our confidence. May the Holy Spirit remind us today to put on the whole armour of God, and never let our guard down. Help us to love one another today, Father God. Help us to inspire someone and sow seeds of kindness into the hearts of others. Father, heal those who are sick this day, from all disease; we bring all sickness to your feet knowing that there's power in your hands. You are the greatest physician, and there's nothing hard for you to do. Restore health to their bodies so they may be how you made us. We declare this morning by your blood they shall be healed. Give their families the comfort and peace they deserve. In Jesus' mighty name we pray... THANK GOD...

Amen.

NOTES

King Jesus, we thank you for raising our heads up to another beautiful day; you're good and your mercies endure forever. We ask that you give us a clear mindset with open ears to hear your voice, and lead and guide us in the way we should go. Teach us to pay close attention to the Holy Spirit that you bring to us, so that our lives can change for the better. Father, we trust you with our lives, and we leave it in your hands. Help us to stay close to you today so that we can hear your voice. Help those who are afraid and anxious because of these difficult days we are living in. We pray for a special blessing over their lives; wrap them in your arms, ease their fears, give them hope, and remind them of your great love for them. Forgive us of anything that we will do today that is not pleasing in your sight, and help us to do right. We are more than conquerors, we are loved, we are special, we are valuable, and we are your children. You take good care of your own, and we trust and believe in you. We give your name all the praise, honour, and glory. In Jesus' name we pray... THANK GOD...

Amen.

NOTES

5. *Thank You for Your Mercy*

Heavenly Father, we love you, praise and glorify you. Thank you for your mercy that woke us up this morning, and for bringing us to the end of another week. Father God, you are worthy to be praised; help us to focus on you first and foremost each day, giving you thanks and praise, and for seeking all that is above. Give us your supernatural strength to face this day. We declare that today, with your strength we can defeat the enemy, we can walk in victory, and defeat sin. Let your spirit encamp around us, Lord Jesus. We ask for your protection today over our lives, our children, our families, our friends, our neighbours, and even our enemies. Keep them safe in the palm of your hand. Father, you are a God who delivers and is ever faithful, and we will cast all our cares to you. You are a God who never sleeps nor slumbers, there's no one like you. Help us to walk with you, and walk by faith, not by sight. Help us to live our life in a way that honours and pleases you. Let our hearts not be afraid, because we know you are with us. Father God, we are so grateful for your love, your never-ending mercy, for your amazing grace, and we will forever trust in you and your word. In Jesus' mighty name we pray... THANK GOD...

Amen.

NOTES

Week Forty-Nine

1. Our Faith is in You

King Jesus, as we wake up this morning, we thank you first and foremost for giving us life. We thank you for the sacrifice you have made for us, for dying on the cross, all so that we could be saved. Lord Jesus, we give you all the praise and glory for bringing us to a brand new week, we thank you for keeping us safe throughout all we have been through this year. We ask that you grant us the strength to remain at your side, draw us closer and closer to you. May the Holy Spirit keep us from falling, cover us and seal us with your blood. Lord, give us a heart so that we may put away all selfishness, and wicked desires. Help us to live our life for you and no one else, purge our hearts of anything that displeases you, and draw us to righteousness, pureness, and things that are above and not of this world. Lord, you are our keeper, our hiding place, and our faith is in you. Watch over us, our families, and our friends. Lord, as we start each day of this week, let us put you first and foremost in all that we do. We abide under your shadow, and your divine care. Thank you, Father God, that your grace is sufficient, and that no matter where we go, or what we do you have promised to be with us, in and through all things. In Jesus' holy and precious name we pray.... THANK GOD...

Amen.

NOTES

Father, in the name of Jesus, we come to you on bended knee, with our heart humble to you this morning, giving you thanks and praise. We lift up your name above all today. Jesus, Emmanuel, our coming Father, we thank you for loading us with triumph because the spirit of Christ Jesus is in our lives, and you are our hope and glory. Help us to never take this precious gift of life for granted. We thank you for being able to bring us peace even in these turbulent times. Everything we survive is because of you. Help us to keep our eyes and mind on you, Lord Jesus. May you continue to bless, heal, and keep us sheltered under the shadow of your wings. Send your angels to keep our enemies at bay. We walk today in your power knowing that all things are possible with you. Restore us for your glory, and increase your love in us, so we can love others. We bless your precious and holy name for listening to our prayers. THANK GOD...

Amen.

NOTES

_____

_____

_____

_____

_____

Lord Jesus, we thank you for another beautiful day. Those who didn't make it this morning, Lord, bless their soul and let them be at peace with you. Comfort their families, and let them know you are with them. We thank you for your strength, grace, mercy, power, love and favour. We thank you for taking good care of our hearts. Today we hand over our prayers, and all our needs to you, so that your will can be done in our lives. Surround each and every one of us with your ever-abiding presence, and please manifest your miraculous and powerful way to help us through all things beyond our control. Fill us with your strength, and give us the courage needed to face all difficulties ahead. Help us to stay strong in you and our faith, because your name is stronger than any sickness, more powerful than darkness, and bigger than any mountain. We stand today and proclaim your name, Jesus. THANK GOD...

Amen.

NOTES

4. We Lift Your Name on High

Heavenly Father, thank you for another day of sunrise. Only you can do it, Father God. We love you for your mercy that never fails us; from the moment that we wake up until we lay our heads down, Lord, we will speak of your goodness. Help us to anchor ourselves in you today, teach us to stand strong in you, and choose the path and the way you want us to walk, because you are our strength and our shield. Thank you for your hand of blessings on every area of our lives. We declare that our days of thriving have begun, as we continue to put our faith and trust in you alone. You are worthy of being exalted, and we lift your name on high. All the glory be unto you. In Jesus' name we pray... THANK GOD...

Amen.

NOTES

5. Almighty God, We Sing Your Praises

Almighty God, we adore, and sing your praises. Thank you, Lord Jesus, for not rejecting us, and for loving us enough to die for our sins, even though we don't deserve it. If we are rejected by this world let it be, because we are standing for your word. We are children of God, and we are grateful through your grace and mercy. We can always rely on you, Lord Jesus, we count on you to remain loving. In you, Lord, there is no condemnation, fear, nor confusion. We welcome the Holy Spirit, the helper, comforter, the advocate counsellor. We pray that the Holy Spirit be our strength. We praise you, Father, as when we are broken-hearted you are near to us. Help us to get back to intimacy with you. Help us to manifest our love for each other, so that you will continue to bless us knowing that your love is in us. Whatever we face today and this weekend, we know we can count on you to deliver. In Jesus' precious name... THANK GOD...

Amen.

NOTES

Week Fifty

1. Rain on Us Your Blessings

Heavenly Father, thank you for giving us life, and making everything new. Thank you for your joy, peace and deliverance. Father God, as we come to another new week, rain on us your blessings today and throughout the coming days. Thank you for your protection, grace, and mercy and for bringing us this far. We would have never made it without you. King Jesus, we know our help comes from you, who made Heaven and Earth. We pray for everyone under the sound of our voice. May they be drawn to your presence, and dwell in the secret place of the most high. We ask today that you forgive us for our sins, and we ask that you count not our transgressions but rather our tears of repentance. Help us to worship you, because you are worthy. Strengthen us today, Lord, help us to encourage each other in the faith, be our strong tower, our shade, and resting place, as your Holy Spirit continues to lead. Bless our hearts and bring us total healing. We appreciate you today, Lord Jesus, knowing that you have fought and won our battles for us. Father, we never want to take your goodness for granted. We ask that you continue to help us. Produce a harvest for us today, Father God. We give you all the glory, honour, and praise. In Jesus' precious and holy name we pray... THANK GOD...

Amen.

NOTES

2. In Your Strong Hands We Place Our Day

Dear Lord, we thank you for this day to be glad and rejoice in it. Help us to accept and enjoy all that it holds. We ask that you please help us to focus more on you, and all that your word brings. Lord, your word says in Psalms 119:105: "Your word is a lamp to my feet, and a light to my path." Help us to anchor our faith in you at all times, Father, and trust in no one but you. Deliver us from all fear and doubt, and help us to hear your voice clearly so that we can walk with you in peace and freedom. Show us by your Holy Spirit what to speak over our lives today, and the lives of our families and friends. In your strong hands we place our day, asking and depending on the Holy Spirit to light and guide our way. In Jesus' name we pray...THANK GOD...

Amen.

NOTES

_____

_____

_____

_____

_____

_____

Heavenly Father, creator of all things, we thank you for the resurrection of your son Jesus Christ. We thank you for the resurrection power that is working in our lives. Thank you for another seven days, and the love you have for us. Lord, we ask today that you release the resurrection power to perform miracles in our lives, and grant us breakthroughs in every aspect in our lives, so that we can overcome all forces of darkness. We pray that your resurrection power will release us from any sickness, fear or anything that does not bring joy to our lives. Open the doors of prosperity to us. As the stone was rolled away, roll away any obstacles that will rise against our fruitfulness. Lord, bring to life anything that is dead in our families, and bring us together in love and harmony. We declare we will be walking in newness by your divine resurrection, through new doors of divine opportunities in Jesus' name. We are overcomers and achievers because the resurrection of Jesus is at work in our lives. Thank you for every promise that's in your word. You are good, and you have done glorious things. Let everything we do today and this coming week be of glory to you, and as a testimony of your greatness in our lives. We are blessed and highly favoured because the glory of God is all over us. Rise up in us today, in our homes, Lord Jesus, you are not dead, you are alive.THANK GOD...

Amen.

NOTES

Father, in the name of Jesus, we thank you for waking us up to another day. This is the day you have made and we will be glad and rejoice in it. We thank you for redeeming us with your precious blood, calling us out of darkness into your precious light. All our blessings are from you, Father God. We thank you for all that you have done, and for what you are going to do for us today and the rest of this week. Father, you are faithful, and we ask that you faithfully move into our lives, and the lives of everyone under the sound of our voice this morning. You know the things that each of us are in need of, and we know that you are faithful, and provide us with all that we need. We have no one to turn to but you; you are our good, good Father. Heal, strengthen, and deliver us. You are a God who can do all things, there's nothing too hard for you to do. Bless our going out and coming in this day, keep us in the centre of your will and the palm of your hand. Help us to remember that as we show simple acts of kindness, we are messengers of God's love. Draw us closer to you today, as the Holy Spirit continues to lead our way. In Jesus' name we pray... THANK GOD...

Amen.

NOTES

Loving and Righteous Father, we declare your goodness today. We will send the devil and his angels back to the pit today because he's defeated. Victory is ours today. Lord Jesus, we love you, and we thank you for seeing the value in us. Help us to see the value that you see, help us to look through your eyes, and speak life over our lives, children, grandchildren, families and friends. Allow your presence to be tangible and surround us today. Lord, we are your children, the children of your kingdom, we serve a mighty, righteous, sovereign, holy God, and we give you glory, honour, and praise. We thank you for healing, deliverance, salvation, and transformation today in the mighty name of Jesus. We give you glory because there's no one greater than you. Fill us with your love, and your joy, let the seed we sow be of you, Father. We know you don't lose any battles, God, and so we thank you for making us winners. We are more than conquerors through Jesus Christ that loves us, and so we give your name all the praise, glory, and honour. In Jesus' mighty name we pray... THANK GOD...

Amen.

NOTES

_____

_____

_____

_____

Week Fifty - One

1. Shine Your Light on Our Path Today

Lord Jesus, we thank you for waking us up to the dawn of another day that you have made, to claim your presence and help. We know that you hear our prayers each and every time we go down on our knees, we have the faith you will answer us in your perfect time. You are so faithful, Lord. You told us that "where your love is, there's no fear, because your perfect love drives out all fear."(1 John 4:18) Today we ask that you bind the works of the enemy, and set us free from fear and anxiety. Father God, we believe you will fight all our battles, so help us to cast all our cares upon your shoulder today. Please walk with us and shine your light on our paths daily, making it brighter and easier for us to follow. Be our strength and saviour in and through all things that we are facing. Help us to listen, follow, seek, serve, trust, and rest in you in the mighty name of Jesus. Satan, you are defeated today, like you were yesterday, and you will be tomorrow. You have no place, power or authority over our lives. We declare that today is going to be a great day, in Jesus' mighty name we pray... THANK GOD...

Amen.

NOTES

Father, in the mighty name of Jesus, we praise, and thank you for waking us up to another day. Father, you are so good, gracious, loving and merciful. Father God, help us not to forget how much you love and care for us. As we begin this new day, we are thankful for all that you have planned for us. We don't know what this day will bring, but we ask for your strength to face it and surrender ourselves to you. Give us the wisdom to discern what is good for us and what is not, and to choose according to your will. Mighty God, heal those who are broken hearted, and turn the sadness into joy, let your goodness be upon all that you have made. Father, we thank you for supplying all our needs today and for always making a way where there seems to be none. We place ourselves, our children, our families, and friends under your protective care; guide our step so we are able to make the right decision, and keep you at the centre of it all. We thank you that your compassion never fails. We thank you that your promises are true, and that you are always with us. In Jesus' holy name we pray... THANK GOD...

Amen.

NOTES

_____

_____

_____

_____

3. Another Chance

Gracious and Heavenly Father, we are grateful for the breath of life. Today we know is a gift from you, and it's a day to get things right with you. It's a fresh start to try things we might have failed at again, and we are thankful to you for giving us another chance. Help us not to think that we are better than those who might have not had the chance to see this beautiful day, every second is a blessing from you, Lord Jesus. Help us not to take for granted the life you have given us, and all the blessings you have bestowed upon us, but to give you thanks and praise for everything. May we enjoy our journey, valuing everyone in our lives today. We pray today that you fill our minds with loving thoughts, and may we spend every hour of this day gladly working with you according to your will. Be our present help in all that we do, and show yourself strong on our behalf. Be with us and our loved ones today, Father; in our days of worries and disappointment, help us to be patient within ourselves, and all those who are around us, and when this day is over, we can lay it all at your feet. We thank you now and in advance for your strength, grace, and support when we need it, and for remaining at the forefront of our lives. In Jesus' name we pray... THANK GOD...

Amen.

NOTES

4. *We Kneel Before Your Throne of Grace*

Almighty and Righteous Father, we kneel before your throne of grace this morning. We give you thanks and praise for allowing us to see another day. Equip us and prepare us for everything that we face today, and the rest of this week, Lord Jesus, because we know we can do it with you by our side. Thank you for never leaving us nor forsaking us. Fill us with your Holy Spirit and lead us into a place of peace. Remove our fears, and help us to keep a strong faith and trust in you. We thank you for keeping us from all hurt, harm and dangers; cover everyone under the sound of our voice, and let every step we take be with you. Clear our pathways so that when we fall you will stretch out your hand to guide us on the right and narrow path. Help us not to forget how much you love us, dear Jesus, and how important we are to you. Help us to conform to your will so we can be at peace today. Father, we claim your everlasting presence in our lives. In Jesus' mighty name we pray... THANK GOD...

Amen.

NOTES

Heavenly Father, we give you thanks and praise; you're good and your mercies endure forever. We thank you for protecting us overnight, and we thank you for waking us up to see the light of another day. Father God, we know as we go through this day we will have ups and downs, leaving us at times to wonder which way to turn, but we know through the twists and turns you are right there by our side. Help us to remember you are our refuge and strength, and we belong to you. In you, Father, we will have peace and victory. Grant us the peace that was promised to us, the peace beyond understanding. Empower us as we pray so our minds may focus on you, and we praise you because you have never let us down. There's no one else like you, Heavenly Father. We thank you for being our rock and pillar in all circumstances, because you have a plan for our lives. We trust and believe that you will answer us when we call out your name. Father, help us that we may have no fear in this world, but to fear you, Father God. Remove everything that will hinder our growth. Thank you for hearing our prayer, it's in Jesus' name we pray... THANK GOD...

Amen.

NOTES

_____

_____

_____

1. Another Beautiful Day

Dear Heavenly Father, it's another beautiful day, and we thank you for waking us up, and blessing us. We thank you and magnify you because you are faithful and kind. Thank you for being with us through everything that we are going through. We thank you for our life, and all the love you have for us. We thank you for your hand of protection that is upon our life, and we praise you because your protection is extended to our families. Open our eyes of our understanding so that we continue to pray without ceasing. Help us not to pray and call out to you only when it pleases us, open our heart to divine deliverance, and let your Holy Spirit guide us. Help us to seek you always and give us the strength to seek your face continually. Thank you for being an answering God; change and transform our lives, and give us the courage to embrace whatever plans you have for our lives. May you continue to heal our bodies and mend our broken hearts. We bless your name, and give all praise and glory to you, Father God. We thank you for hearing our prayers. In Jesus' name we pray... THANK GOD...

Amen.

NOTES

---

2. When God Is By Your Side, Nothing Is Impossible

Lord Jesus, we give you praise, honour, and glory for waking us up to another glorious day. You lead us beside still water, and you restore our soul. We are on our knees at this present moment because there are some things we can't see until we bow. You are great, you know every plan for our future; deliver us and have your way, Father God. Help us to stay on course and keep us reminded to never cease trusting in you. Keep us with strong faith, and give us the strength and the courage to embrace whatever changes you bestow upon us in this life. As your word says, "no weapon formed against us shall prosper." Father, we know the weapon is formed sometimes, it's pointing us right in our face, but you said it wouldn't prosper, so we thank you for giving us the victory. We pray for everyone this morning under the sound of our voice; give us the strength to keep fighting and hanging on to you. We thank you for walking with us, and leading us on our journey. With a humble heart, we thank you for hearing and answering all our prayers. In Jesus' mighty name we pray... THANK GOD...

Amen.

NOTES

Heavenly Father, we thank you for the start of a new day. As we cement ourselves and everything to you, we know each day you have blessed us to see you are guiding our steps and blessing all those we lift up in our prayers. We honour, praise and worship you because you love your children. Cover us, Father God, and hide us from the counsel of the wicked; cast us not away from your presence, and do not remove your Holy Spirit from us. We pray for your divine covering today. Help us to be wise throughout this day to make wise decisions, and to navigate our life with wisdom. Father, give us the wisdom, knowledge, and understanding that will help us in our daily walk with you. Lord, you are sitting up high and looking down on us today. Open our eyes so we can see what is deeper than what we see on the surface. Open our hearts and fill them with your presence, and the joy that will sink deep into our soul.

May the Holy Spirit cover our children who are going to school today; manifest your presence before them, let them not be distracted by anything that will lead them to danger. We declare that they will be covered by your blood in the mighty name of Jesus. Make your presence felt anew today, make it true for us and this world, as we cast our cares to you. In Jesus' mighty name we pray... THANK GOD...

Amen.

NOTES

4. Melodies from Heaven

Melodies from Heaven rain down on us this morning. Father, we love you and thank you for the mercies and blessings that you bestowed upon us, you are a God of love and compassion. Help us to embrace and rejoice in all that today holds, and be content and be grateful without any complaints. As we go through the unbearable challenges that put pressure on our minds and shoulders today, we ask you to keep our minds focused on you. Whatever we come up against, give us the strength to rebuke the devil in your name, King Jesus, and let the enemy know that he has no power, nor authority over our lives. You are our rock, strength and fortress, and our strong tower. Help us at all times to pour out our hearts to you, because you are our refuge. We thank you that your presence goes with us, and that your joy is never dependent on our circumstances, but it is our true and lasting strength. We thank you for being our peace, and our very present help in times of trouble. Thank you for hearing and answering all our prayers. In Jesus's mighty name we pray... THANK GOD...

Amen.

NOTES

Heavenly Father, we dedicate this day to you. You are a mighty God, a God who loves us and has proven your love in so many ways. Thank you for another day to serve and follow you. Father, we thank you and praise you for your many promises that provide us with hope and a sense of security. We praise you and appreciate all the times you have come to our aid. You are a God who cares, and is present to help us each time we set out on our journey. Be our protection, Father God, make a way for us, and bring peace to the storms we face, in our families, amongst our friends, and even in our job. Shield and protect us, because we know our help comes from you, the Lord who created Heaven and Earth. We invite you to be close to us as we draw closer to you. You are our hiding place and you will protect us from trouble. As we begin this day, and we end this day, may we do so under your protection and divine care. Father God, we give you all the glory, and we thank you for preserving our soul throughout this day and weekend ahead. Let everything we do bring honour to you in the mighty and powerful name of Jesus Christ. THANK GOD...

Amen.

NOTES

About the Author

"I SERVE A GOD WHO MAKES ALL THINGS POSSIBLE" (2 Corinthians 5:17)

Lavern was born in Kingston, Jamaica, and now resides in the United Kingdom. She is the mother of four grown children, a businesswoman, and a staunch believer in Jesus Christ, our Lord and Saviour. Consistently, she has been sending a daily prayer each morning to her family and friends on Whatsapp. It is her way of keeping their spiritual roots hydrated.

Made in United States
Orlando, FL
29 March 2024